Taxcafe.co.uk Tax Guides

Non Resident & Offshore Tax Planning

By Lee Hadnum LLB ACA CTA

Important Legal Notices:

TAXCafe[TM]
TAX GUIDE - "Non Resident & Offshore Tax Planning"

Published by:
Taxcafe UK Limited
214 High St
Kirkcaldy KY1 1JT
Tel: (0044) 01592 560081
Email: team@taxcafe.co.uk

First Edition, April 2003
Second Edition, December 2003
Third Edition, March 2004

ISBN 1 904608 10 8

Disclaimer
Before reading or relying on the content of this Tax Guide please read carefully the disclaimer on the last page which applies. If you have any queries then please contact the publisher at team@taxcafe.co.uk.

About The Author

Lee Hadnum is a key member of the Taxcafe.co.uk team. Apart from authoring a number of our tax guides, he also provides personalised tax advice through our popular Question & Answer Service, a role he carries out with a great deal of enthusiasm and professionalism.

Lee is a rarity among tax advisers having both legal AND chartered accountancy qualifications. After qualifying as a prize winner in the Institute of Chartered Accountants entrance exams, he went on to become a Chartered Tax Adviser (CTA).

Having worked in Ernst & Young's tax department for a number of years, Lee decided to start his own tax consulting firm, specialising in capital gains tax, inheritance tax and business tax planning.

He also tutors at a number of accountancy colleges in the north-west of England.

Whenever he has spare time Lee enjoys DIY, walking and travelling.

If you would like further advice, Lee can be contacted directly at lee@taxcafe.co.uk

Nick Braun, Managing Director, Taxcafe UK Limited

Contents

Chapter 1

Introduction

This guide is designed to help those living or working abroad pay less tax on their UK income and investments. It also contains important information for those who live in the UK but wish to use the offshore tax rules to shelter their income and gains from the taxman.

This is an important and sophisticated area of tax planning. Moving yourself or your assets abroad is in many respects the ultimate form of tax avoidance and in some cases it is possible to reduce your tax bill to zero. However, there are also many traps to avoid and pitfalls to negotiate.

This publication highlights some of the key tax-planning opportunities and dangers, focusing on the UK's four major taxes: income tax, capital gains tax, inheritance tax and corporation tax.

Throughout we have tried to keep tax jargon to a minimum and illustrate the main points with examples.

A significant portion of the guide is devoted to the potential emigrant - individuals who are considering moving overseas and have heard that this may bring with it substantial tax benefits.

We look at the tax-saving opportunitites, as well as the practical steps and dangers to bear in mind, when considering a move abroad.

In Chapter 2 we explain the concept of 'non residence' which has a huge effect on the amount of income tax and capital gains tax you pay. We also explain the concept of 'domicile' as there are a number of special rules for individuals who are UK resident but not UK domiciled. Domicile is also crucial when it comes to inheritance tax planning.

In Chapter 3 we list the steps you need to take to convince the taxman that you are non-resident and discuss some of the traps the authorities have set to catch 'phoney emigrants'.

Chapters 4, 5 and 6 take a detailed look at income tax, capital gains tax and inheritance tax-planning strategies for non-residents. The information contained in these chapters is extremely important for any would-be tax exile or emigrant and should be read carefully.

In Chapter 7 we focus our attention on 'foreign nationals' living and working in the UK and explain how they can use their special status to obtain tax savings.

In Chapter 8 we look at the income tax, capital gains tax and inheritance tax implications of working and travelling overseas as, aside from the 'permanent emigrant', many of you reading this may be considering an overseas posting. After reading this guide you should have a clear understanding of how working abroad will affect your UK tax position.

Chapter 9 explains how you can use a number of reliefs to avoid being taxed twice - once in the UK and again in another country.

Offshore trusts and offshore companies are sometimes viewed as the preserve of the very wealthy. This is not necessarily the case and we have outlined in Chapters 10 and 11 how these structures can help you save tax and how to avoid the detailed tax anti-avoidance rules.

Reducing tax on property investments is a top priority for many UK residents and non-residents. The guide contains numerous examples with a 'property theme' and in Chapter 12 we take a closer look at how non-resident and non-domiciled investors should structure their property purchases.

Your residence status is often the critical factor when it comes to paying both UK and foreign taxes. But what if you can avoid being resident in ANY country? In Chapter 13 we take a brief look at how you can become a 'tax nomad' and avoid both UK and overseas taxes.

Throughout this guide we have attempted to identify practical steps that can be taken to mitigate any UK tax, although the tax regime of any relevant overseas country should also be borne in mind. This is where double tax treaties come in. In Chapter 14 we explain the importance of these treaties in further detail.

Finally, Chapter 15 takes an in-depth look at buying property abroad and how to plan your affairs to avoid both UK and overseas income tax and capital gains tax.

We occasionally use some abbreviations. In particular, capital gains tax may be referred to as CGT and inheritance tax as IHT.

A lot of expat and offshore tax planning depends on getting dates and timing right. So many of the examples are based on specific tax years.

Remember that the UK tax year runs from April 6th to April 5th.

The tax year running from April 6th 2004 to April 5th 2005 may be referred to as the 2004-2005 tax year or just 04-05.

Chapter 2

Residence, Ordinary Residence & Domicile

2.1 Why Do Residence & Domicile Matter?

The short answer is, they affect the amount of tax you have to pay.

UK residents who are also UK domiciled (we'll explain domicile later) have to pay UK income tax and capital gains tax on their 'worldwide income and gains'. In other words, no matter where in the world your assets are located or in what country your income is earned, it all falls into the UK tax net.

Those who are UK resident but non-UK domiciled are only subject to UK income tax on income from foreign assets *when they bring it into the UK*.

If you are a non-resident you do not have to pay UK tax on *non-UK income*. However, you still have to pay UK tax on your UK salary, business profits (if the business is carried out in the UK), pension income and investment income. There are, however, some special rules that can reduce the tax non-residents pay on any UK income.

Capital gains tax depends on both your residence and 'ordinary residence'. If you cease to be resident in the UK without also ceasing to be ordinarily resident here, you will remain liable to UK capital gains tax in respect of gains on your worldwide assets.

If an individual ceases to be both resident and ordinarily resident, he is *outside the scope of UK capital gains tax*, even on UK assets.

So clearly your residence and domicile have a huge effect on the size of your UK tax bill. The crucial question is how do you qualify for these reliefs and exemptions?

2.2   Becoming Non-Resident

There is no formal legal definition of 'residence'. Inland Revenue's practice - based on a mixture of statute and court decisions - is to regard you as resident in the UK during a tax year if :

- You spend 183 days or more in the UK during the tax year, or

- Although here for less than 183 days, you have spent more than 90 days per year in the country over the past four years (taken as an average). You will then be classed as UK resident from the fifth year.

These rules have no statutory force and are guidance only. For example, an individual who regularly returns to the UK for 87 days per tax year may still be regarded as UK resident.

A person can also be resident in two countries at the same time. It is therefore not possible to escape UK residence by arguing that you are resident elsewhere.

It is important to note that UK residence is a question of fact and not intention. Therefore although you may intend to leave before the 183-day limit, if you are forced to remain in the UK as a result of exceptional circumstances you will nevertheless be regarded as UK resident.

(On a technical note, in strict terms when calculating the number of days an individual spends in the UK, the hours that he is in this country on the days of arrival and departure should be taken into account. However, in practice Inland Revenue allows the days of arrival and departure to be ignored, although if the tax at stake is significant, it would be unwise to depend too heavily on this practice.)

2.3 The Importance of 'Ordinary Residence'

Even if you qualify as non-resident you may still fall into the taxman's clutches by being classified as *UK ordinarily resident*.

There is also no statutory test of ordinary residence. You will be classified as a UK ordinary resident if the UK is your 'normal place of residence'.

On leaving the country you will continue to be regarded as UK ordinary resident unless you go abroad with the intention of taking up permanent residence overseas.

Inland Revenue normally interprets 'permanent' to mean three years or more.

It is therefore possible to be non-UK resident but UK ordinarily resident. This would occur, for example, where you go abroad for a long holiday and do not return to the UK during a particular tax year. You will continue to be classed as UK ordinary resident until you can show that you have taken up a permanent residence elsewhere.

The consequence of being classed as not UK ordinary resident is that you will not have to pay UK capital gains tax on your worldwide capital gains.

A person who is UK resident under the 183-day test may not necessarily be UK ordinary resident. Such a person would then have to pay tax on overseas income and gains that are brought into the UK (this applies for Commonwealth and Irish citizens). However, a person who is UK resident as a result of the 90-day test would find it difficult to argue that he or she is not also UK ordinary resident and therefore worldwide income and gains would be taxed as they arise, not just when brought into the UK.

One factor that is likely to be taken into account in assessing ordinary residence is whether you continue to own and occupy property in the UK - in particular, where the use or occupation of the property is combined with other factors, such as regular visits to the UK only slightly below the 90-day average. This will be persuasive evidence that you have not taken up a permanent residence elsewhere.

However, subject to this, a person who leaves the UK will cease to be UK ordinary resident if he or she establishes non-UK residence for three consecutive tax years.

2.4   Residence in a Nutshell

As you can see, residence issues can be fairly complex. It is useful to consolidate the above before looking at the detailed rules:

- An individual who is UK resident/ordinarily resident and domiciled will be liable to UK tax on his/her worldwide income and gains.

- An individual who is UK resident/ordinarily resident but *not* UK domiciled will generally be liable to UK tax on overseas income/gains only when the income/proceeds are remitted to the UK. This is known as the remittance basis.

- An individual who is UK resident but not ordinarily resident will also be subject to the remittance basis for *overseas* income and gains (provided he or she is a Commonwealth or Irish citizen).

- An individual who is non-resident and not ordinarily resident will be liable to UK income tax on UK source income but will be exempt from UK capital gains tax on all assets (whether situated in the UK or overseas), except for assets used in a UK trade.

Example 1

John who is UK domiciled has purchased a holiday villa in Spain and intends to spend as much time there as possible.

Having purchased it in May 2004 (in other words, during the 2004/2005 tax year) John stays nine months in the villa. In order to supplement his income he is renting out his property in the UK (through a letting agent) and will obtain a small part-time job in a Spanish wine factory, tasting local wines.

From a UK tax perspective he will be regarded as non-UK resident as he has exceeded the 182-day limit. Therefore:

- *His UK source income (in other words, rental income) will be subject to UK income tax.*
- *His overseas income (his income from his part-time job in Spain) will not be subject to UK taxation.*

If Spanish property prices were to suddenly increase, John may decide to take advantage of this and dispose of his Spanish villa in July 2005, for a healthy profit.

As he has not left the UK permanently and he has not yet been non-resident for three complete tax years, he is likely to still be regarded as UK ordinarily resident. This will mean that his profit from the sale of the Spanish villa will be subject to UK capital gains tax (subject to the terms of any double tax treaty - considered later).

Example 2

Johnny, of Australian domicile, makes regular visits to the UK to visit his friends in London. His visits to the UK over the past few tax years have been as follows:

2000/2001   85 days
2001/2002   97 days
2002/2003   110 days
2003/2004   115 days

His annual average visits are (85+97+110+115)/4 = 102 days.
He will therefore be regarded as UK resident from 6 April 2004 and subject to UK tax on his worldwide income and gains, although the remittance basis would apply to his overseas income and gains.

If he has a job in Australia he will not be subject to UK tax if he keeps the income out of the UK. However, to the extent that he brings it into the UK, eg for spending money during his visits, it will be subject to UK tax.

Any amounts that are taxed twice will be entitled to double tax relief (this is explained later in the guide).

It should be noted that if Johnny had any firm intentions, beginning with the commencement of his visits to the UK in 1999, that his visits would be on the above basis, then he would be regarded as UK resident from the date that these intentions were formed.

For example, if Johnny had declared in May 2001 that he would be making substantial visits to the UK in the following tax years and, for example, booked time off work to make the visits, he would be regarded as UK resident from this date.

2.5 Why 'Domicile' is Important for Tax Planning

The concept of 'domicile' is extremely important when it comes to both inheritance tax and overseas tax planning.

It's important to point out that your 'nationality' or 'citizenship' are NOT necessarily the same as your domicile.

You are normally domiciled in the country that you regard as your home – not the place where you happen to be temporarily living. Your domicile is, in a sense, the country that you regard as your true 'homeland' and has frequently been described as the country in which a person intends to die.

It is therefore possible for a person to live in the UK for 40 years yet still remain legally domiciled in another country. Losing your UK domicile is substantially more difficult than losing your UK resident status.

While it is possible to be resident in two countries at the same time, it is only possible to be domiciled in one.

There are three types of domicile:

1. Domicile of Origin

A domicile of origin is acquired when a person is born. Under normal circumstances this is the father's domicile at the date of the child's birth. If the parents are unmarried, it is the mother's domicile that matters.

A domicile of origin continues unless the individual acquires either a domicile of dependency or a domicile of choice (see below). This new domicile will remain in force unless it is abandoned, in which case the domicile of origin is revived.

2. Domicile of Choice

In order to acquire a domicile of choice, a person must voluntarily make a new territory his residence and intend to remain there for the rest of his days - unless and until something occurs to make him change his mind.

Obtaining a domicile of choice is primarily a *question of intent*. However, once such a domicile has been established it is relatively difficult to abandon. It would be necessary for an individual to cease to reside in the country of choice indefinitely. Later on in this guide we list some practical steps that can be taken to help establish a domicile of choice.

3. Domicile of Dependency

This type of domicile only applies to children under the age of 16. A child's domicile of origin is replaced by a domicile of dependency if there is a change in the father's domicile (mother's domicile in the case of unmarried couples). If this happens, the parent's domicile of choice becomes the child's domicile of dependency. The child keeps this domicile unless the child does not live in the territory and never intends to live there. In this case the child's domicile of origin revives.

Example

John was born in Latvia and is regarded as being of Latvian domicile. John went to live in France and successfully established France as his domicile of choice. His son Jack, who was born in Latvia, would also initially have a Latvian domicile of origin. However, he would 'inherit' his father's French domicile. This would become his domicile of dependency. If Jack intends to permanently return to Latvia on his 18th birthday and makes preparations for this, his domicile will revert to his domicile of origin. The domicile of dependency has essentially been changed - by indicating his intention to return to Latvia, the domicile of origin 'reasserts' itself.

2.6 Watch Out for this Inheritance Tax Trap

Inheritance tax issues are dealt with later in the guide. However it is worth noting now that for inheritance tax purposes only there is the concept of 'deemed domicile'. Individuals are deemed to have a UK domicile:

- If they have been UK resident for 17 out of the last 20 years, or
- They have lost their UK domicile in the last three years.

Example

David was born in France, but has been living in the UK since 1960. He has always intended to return to France, and still regards France as his home. For income tax purposes, and under the general law, David is of French domicile.

However, for inheritance tax purposes, he is deemed UK domicile as he has lived in the UK since 1960 and would therefore have been resident for more than 17 years.

Therefore for inheritance tax purposes, David's estate would be subject to UK inheritance tax on his worldwide estate. On his return to France, David would continue to be deemed UK domicile for IHT purposes for three years after leaving the UK.

Chapter 3

How You Can Become Non-Resident & Avoid UK Tax

3.1 What You Stand to Gain

Some people emigrate to soak up the sun and live in an exotic location. Others leave the country to escape the UK taxman. However, it is worth noting that tax rates in most industrialised countries are *higher* than those in the UK. Therefore, if you become non-resident to avoid tax, you may end up jumping out of the frying pan and into the fire!

To achieve a permanent reduction in tax it is often necessary to move to a tax haven or low tax jurisdiction such as Jersey or the Isle of Man.

It should also be noted that a double taxation agreement between the UK and your country of choice could result in your UK income falling outside the scope of UK tax but inside the scope of another country's tax regime. Double taxation agreements are considered in further detail later in the guide.

Before looking at living abroad in further detail, it is useful to remind ourselves of the general rules for income tax, capital gains tax and inheritance tax. The main points can be summarised as follows:

- Income tax is based primarily on residence. If you are resident in the UK, you are normally liable to UK tax on your worldwide income. If you are not resident you are still liable to UK tax on income arising in the UK, but your non-UK income is outside the scope of UK income tax.

- Capital gains tax depends on both residence and ordinary residence. If you cease to be resident in the UK without also ceasing to be ordinarily resident here, you will remain liable to UK capital gains tax in respect of gains on your worldwide assets. If you cease to be both resident and ordinarily resident, you are outside the scope of UK capital gains tax, even on UK assets.

- Inheritance tax is based on domicile. If a person is domiciled in the UK he is liable to UK inheritance tax on his worldwide assets even though he may be both resident and ordinarily resident in another country. If a person is not domiciled here, he is generally liable to inheritance tax on his UK assets only. (The deemed domicile rules outlined earlier should, however, be considered.)

Example 1
Brian is UK resident, ordinarily resident and domiciled during the 2004/2005 tax year. He will be liable to UK income tax on his worldwide income, UK capital gains tax on his worldwide gains and UK inheritance tax on his worldwide estate.

Example 2

Peter is UK non-resident and UK non-domiciled. He will still be liable to UK income tax on his UK income, although his overseas income will be outside the scope of UK income tax. On the assumption that he will remain non-resident for at least five complete tax years (see Chapter 5 on capital gains tax), Peter will not be liable to UK capital gains tax on either his UK or overseas gains. As he is non-UK domiciled he will be liable to UK inheritance tax on his UK estate - his overseas assets will be outside the scope of UK inheritance tax.

Example 3

David is UK non-resident but UK domiciled. He will be liable to UK income tax on any UK source income, exempt from UK capital gains tax on any gains yet he will still be liable for UK inheritance tax on his worldwide estate.

3.2 Convincing the Taxman You Are Non-Resident

Chapter 2 outlined the current Inland Revenue rules regarding residence and domicile. While it is vital to understand the basic principles, what most people want to know is how they can become non-resident and reduce their exposure to UK taxes. We will look here at the practical steps that should be taken to help strengthen a claim for non-residence (domicile issues are looked at in detail later).

Selling Your Home

You should consider selling your UK house before leaving the country, assuming that any gain is covered by the Principal Private Residence relief and therefore escapes capital gains tax. If you are unsure whether this relief applies, further advice should be taken.

If the house cannot be sold before departure, you should try not to return to the UK at all until after it has been disposed of and is no longer available for you to use. An alternative to selling the house is to let it. However, care needs to be taken with this - depending on the circumstances, the taxman could argue that keeping property in the UK casts doubt on your intention to leave the country permanently.

This is particularly dangerous where there is a short-term lease, for example under four years, as the Inland Revenue could then argue that possession would be obtained within three years of departure. In such circumstances it would be advisable to obtain any evidence that the short-term let was made for commercial reasons and that you intend to be overseas for at least four years.

Returning to the UK
You should try to not return to the UK at any time between your departure and the following 5th April, in other words, the tax year of departure. If you do, Inland Revenue is unlikely to accept that you have left the country permanently until after the last such visit.

You should try not to return to the UK at any time during the year of assessment following that in which you emigrate, in other words, the tax year following departure. It would then be unlikely that Inland Revenue could class you as UK resident.

This is important as it shows a firm intention to break with this country. If you wish to visit the UK during your first full tax year abroad it would not be fatal to your emigration claim, but any visits should be as few as possible and for short periods.

If you were to visit for up to three months (as you are theoretically able to do without being classified as UK resident under the 90-day test) this is likely to cast doubt on whether you really intended to live permanently abroad. Inland Revenue could argue that you should be regarded as UK ordinarily resident and subject to UK capital gains tax on disposals of your worldwide assets.

It is also wise to keep a record of the reasons for the visits to the UK as these can demonstrate that any visits were unconnected with your 'ongoing lifestyle'.

The emigrant should try to limit visits to the UK in the next two years. Visits during the part year of departure and the three tax years following departure are what will primarily influence the taxman's views on your residence status. If such visits are minimal there are unlikely to be problems.

Buying a Property Abroad

You should buy or rent a property in another country as soon as possible. This will have an impact on your ordinary residence status as it will show a permanent intention to move abroad.

Many of the above steps are also useful when considering the emigrant's domicile.

3.3 How to Avoid Timing Traps

Strictly, the decision as to whether you are resident/ordinarily resident needs to be made for an entire tax year. In other words, you are not normally resident for part of a tax year.

Example 1
Keith is present in the UK from 6 April 2004 to 7 October 2004 (185 days). He would be resident in the UK for the entire 2004/2005 tax year.

In practice, an exception is made to this rule where a person leaves the UK to take up a 'permanent' residence elsewhere. Such a person is regarded as resident in the UK from 6 April to the date of his departure. In other words, rather than being regarded as UK resident for the whole of the tax year, the individual will be regarded as non-resident for the period that he is overseas.

This treatment is known as 'split year' treatment and is allowed by way of an Inland Revenue concession. It should be noted that because this is a concession, if large amounts of tax are at stake, it may be unwise to rely too heavily on it.

Example 2
John left the UK permanently on 1 April 2005. He received a large overseas dividend on 3 April 2005. On a strict legal perspective, John would be UK resident for the whole of the 2004/2005 tax year and therefore the dividend would be subject to UK income tax.

However, as John has left the UK permanently (and has evidence to support this) the split year treatment would treat John as non-resident for the period 1 April to 5 April and therefore no UK income tax would be due on the overseas income.

In practice, as Inland Revenue is entitled to refuse the benefit of the concession and could tax the dividend, it would be beneficial if possible to arrange for the dividend to be paid in the following tax year, in other words, from 6 April 2005.

The split year treatment is unlikely to be applied for capital gains tax purposes, unless the individual has been UK resident and ordinarily resident for less than four years.

3.4 How the Taxman Decides Residence Status

When you leave the country you will provisionally be treated as ceasing to be resident and ordinarily resident in the UK from the day of departure - providing you can produce evidence to show that you intend to live permanently abroad for at least three years.

What can be regarded as acceptable evidence clearly depends on the particular facts. If you sell your UK property and purchase a new overseas property, this is suggestive of an intention to live permanently overseas. By contrast, if the UK property remains furnished and unlet, this could be regarded as evidence that you have not decided to make a permanent move.

If you cannot produce evidence at the date of departure, the Inland Revenue will normally treat you as remaining UK resident and ordinarily resident. After a period of three years they will review your position in order to make a final decision on whether you ceased to be resident and ordinarily resident in the UK at the date of departure.

They will look closely at the length of any visits to the UK and therefore, even though you may have intended to emigrate permanently, if something subsequently happened to persuade you to resume UK residence, it would be very difficult to persuade the tax authorities that you left the UK with the intention of emigrating permanently.

The Inland Revenue's approach is to treat an individual's residence/domicile as another entry in the tax return. They will therefore either accept your claim or look into it further, as with any other entry on your return. It is possible to obtain an informal review of your status by submitting a form P85 (before you submit your tax return)

stating that you regard yourself as non-resident from a certain date. The Inland Revenue will then have the opportunity to respond with a request for further information. It should be noted that the Inland Revenue is not legally bound under this procedure, although in practice they would be unlikely to enquire into the non-residency if they have previously agreed that an emigrant is non-resident, provided full information was provided to them. This therefore shows the importance of disclosing all relevant information to the taxman.

Chapter 4

How to Avoid UK Income Tax

4.1 Introduction

The basic rule is that UK residents are taxed on their *worldwide income*. Non-residents are only taxed on their *UK income*.

A person leaving the country to avoid income tax needs to remember that the UK, like most countries, claims the right to tax income arising in the UK, irrespective of whether it is earned by a resident or a non-resident.

You also need to take account of double tax treaties. A double tax treaty is an agreement between two countries that determines which country can tax which income, where an individual is a resident of both countries. The rules laid out in these treaties override the domestic tax legislation.

Most double taxation agreements provide for a substantial degree of exemption from UK tax for residents of treaty countries. This means the income is not taxed in the UK but is taxed in the other country. The drawback with this set-up is that most treaties are with countries with tax systems similar to our own - there are very few treaties with tax havens. Double tax treaties are discussed in more detail later in the guide.

So what can you do to minimise your UK income tax bill?

One solution is to dispose of all assets that generate UK income. Such a disposal would also provide evidence of your intention to move abroad permanently and would help to demonstrate that you are not UK ordinarily resident. Of course, the capital gains tax consequences of selling your assets would also have to be considered (see Chapter 5, *How to Avoid UK Capital Gains Tax*).

If selling your assets is not viable, it is worth noting that, apart from rental income, **most UK investment income received by non-residents is not liable to additional tax beyond what is deducted at source**. Let's take a closer look at the tax treatment of different types of investment income:

4.2   Rental Income

Non-residents have to pay tax on rental income from UK properties. There is a 20% withholding tax on the rent. If a firm of letting agents looks after your property, they are responsible for paying the withheld income tax to Inland Revenue. Where there is no letting agent, it is the responsibility of the tenant. The letting agent/tenant has to account for this basic rate tax each quarter.

Where a tenant's gross rent is less than £100 per week, there is no requirement to deduct tax unless instructed to do so by Inland Revenue.

Any tax withheld is allowed as a credit against your eventual UK tax liability calculated on your self assessment tax return.

Non-residents can also obtain permission to self assess any UK tax liability. This option avoids the withholding tax and is applied for by using form 'NRL1'. Separate forms must be submitted for jointly held properties.

Inland Revenue will generally give its approval providing:

- Your tax affairs are up to date; or
- You do not expect to be liable for any UK tax; or
- You have never had any UK tax obligations.

The tax on the profits of the rental business is then calculated on the self assessment tax return, with any income tax liability usually payable by the 31st January following the end of the tax year.

It is still possible to obtain a deduction for qualifying loan interest as long as it has been incurred 'wholly and exclusively' in relation to the rental income.

4.3 Interest & Royalties

Interest and royalties paid overseas from the UK are subject to a 20% withholding tax, with no further liability - **in other words, no higher rate tax is payable**.

If you are not ordinarily resident in the UK you can apply to have your interest paid without any tax deducted, by completing a 'not ordinarily resident' declaration (form 'R105'). It should be noted that the interest is still subject to UK tax and would have to be accounted for in the annual tax return.

It may be worthwile considering whether to transfer any cash in a UK bank account to an overseas account.

There would be no capital gains tax implications (as cash is not a chargeable asset for capital gains tax purposes) and no UK tax would be payable on your interest, provided you are non-resident.

And what about ISAs? Individuals can only make payments into Individual Savings Accounts (ISAs) if they are UK resident and ordinarily resident. So, for example, an individual who works abroad for a complete tax year and is regarded as non-resident will not be able to make ISA contributions during the period of non-residency. However, it's worth holding on to your existing ISAs as you will continue to enjoy the tax benefits no matter how long you live abroad.

There is also a special rule for investments in Government bonds (also known as gilts). Interest from these investments is completely tax free if you are non resident.

4.4 Dividends

There is no withholding tax on dividends, and for UK tax purposes, there will be no higher rate income tax charge. All dividends are treated as having suffered a 10% tax charge at source and for non-UK residents, this will satsify any basic rate income tax liability, so effectively dividend income is tax free in your hands.

Just as for UK residents, the 10% 'deemed' tax credit cannot give rise to a repayment of income tax.

However, depending on the terms of any double taxation agreement, income tax may STILL be payable in the home country.

4.5 Pension Income

The general rules applying to investment income also apply to pension income.

A UK resident/ordinarily resident *and* domiciled individual is subject to UK income tax on UK and overseas pensions. However there is one key tax relief. A 10% deduction is given against all *overseas* pension income.
This means that such an individual is only taxed on 90% of his or her pension payments.

If the pensioner is *non-domiciled* and is using the remittance basis to account for overseas income, then the 10% deduction will not be available.

Such a pensioner is fully liable to to UK tax on UK pensions but overseas pensions will only be taxed when remitted to the UK, and the 10% deduction is not available.
If you are *non-UK resident* you will not pay UK tax on any overseas pensions.

4.6   Employment Income

Employment income is taxed under something called Schedule E. There are three 'cases' of Schedule E.

Case I
This applies to individuals who are UK resident and ordinarily resident and covers both UK and foreign work duties.

The tax charge is on a receipts basis and the full amount of worldwide emoluments/salary is subject to UK income tax, except for one specific situation that falls within Case III (below).

Case II
This applies to non-resident individuals, or individuals resident but not ordinarily resident in the UK and covers only salary arising from UK duties.

Case III
This applies where an employee is either

- Resident but not ordinarily resident in the UK or

- The employee is UK resident/ordinarily resident but is of foreign domicile, works for a foreign employer and performs all duties outside of the UK.

In either of these cases the overseas salary can be assessed on a remittance basis, and is only subject to UK income tax when received in the UK.

Examples
David, of Jamaican domicile, has been working in the UK for a computer company. He is UK resident and will be fully taxed on his employment income under Schedule E, Case I.

Robert is a non-resident, yet he earns a salary from being a director of a UK company and pays regular visits to the UK head office throughout the year (but stays within the 90-day limit). He will be subject to income tax on his UK employment income under Schedule E, Case II. As he is non-resident, any overseas income will be exempt from UK income tax.

Peter, UK resident but non-UK domiciled, is to work overseas for four months for an overseas subsidiary of his UK employer.

The duties of the employment will be performed wholly abroad. He will be taxed on his overseas employment income under Schedule E, Case III on a remittance basis - in other words he is subject to UK tax on income that is brought into the UK.

It is therefore important to understand the definition of UK and overseas duties.

A non-UK resident individual is not subject to UK income tax on salary received for duties performed wholly abroad. Any 'incidental duties' performed in the UK will not create a problem, provided these duties are clearly ancillary or subordinate to the overseas employment, eg going back to to the UK for meetings at head office.

Example

Freddy has been offered a secondment to the Paris office of his employer. It is proposed that this is from 4 April 2004 - 3 April 2006. Freddy is happy with this as he is likely to be regarded as non-resident and not ordinarily resident from the date of his departure.

Freddy must then look at the duties that he will be undertaking, as it is the earnings from the overseas employment that are exempt from UK income tax. Let's assume Freddy's job is to source French products that may be in demand from the British market. If as part of his role he is to return to the UK on a monthly basis and produce and advise on the production and marketing of these products, it may be that these duties are not incidental to the overseas employment, particularly if he is to spend, say, one week each month in the UK advising on this. If Inland Revenue successfully argued the case, the employment income would need to be apportioned between UK and overseas income, with the UK income subject to UK income tax.

An emigrant who remains a Commonwealth citizen is entitled to claim the UK personal allowance, which is £4,745 for the 2004/05 tax year. You may, however, prefer not to make a claim for this allowance. Any claim made is usually dealt with by the Centre for Non Residents which could reconsider on an annual basis whether or not you are UK resident. This could be costly for you in terms of both time and money.

4.7   UK Social Security Contributions

This is a tremendously complex area. However, generally no social security contributions are required to be paid by an individual who ceases to be ordinarily resident for social security purposes and who is paid by an overseas employer.

Where an individual is seconded abroad Class 1 contributions are normally payable for 12 months after departure.

4.8   Pension Planning

We take a closer look at working abroad later on. However, where an individual goes to work overseas there are a few issues to bear in mind as regards pensions:

- Will any benefits already accrued in a UK scheme be capable of being transferred into an overseas scheme?
- If you remain a member of a UK scheme, will any employer and employee contributions be taxed/tax deductible?

An individual sent overseas for a long period of service may wish to join a pension fund established in the overseas country.

In order to transfer benefits from an existing UK scheme the overseas scheme must be approved by the UK pensions office. The UK has special arrangements with the Isle of Man, Jersey, Guernsey and the Republic of Ireland so that approval need not be sought.

For other countries, if approval is not given, contributions to the scheme by the employee will not be tax deductible and he will have to pay tax on any contributions made by the employer (in other words, the employer's contributions will effectively be regarded as 'additional salary').

Alternatively, an employee may go abroad to work for a UK resident employer, and may decide to retain his UK occupational pension scheme. Broadly, where an individual has been seconded abroad and his service overseas is with a subsidiary of the UK employer or a company within the same group, the employee may remain within the occupational pension scheme, provided the overseas employment is not expected to last more than 10 years.

Example

Patrick has been offered an opportunity to work in his UK employer's Milan subsidiary for two years. He has been paying into the employer's occupational pension scheme and wishes to continue doing so.

As the employment is expected to last for two years and the overseas employer is part of the UK group, any pension contributions made by Patrick to his UK occupational scheme will be tax deductible.

Stakeholder pensions

An individual who is UK resident can make contributions of up to £3,600 per year to a stakeholder pension scheme, even if the individual in question has no UK earnings in that year. And what about non-residents? Provided they started the scheme whilst UK resident (otherwise they wouldn't be eligible) they will be allowed to continue the contributions (either at £3,600 per annum or based on earnings in the year of departure) for a further five tax years (whilst non-resident).

4.9 Out of the Frying Pan into the Fire

A key problem is that most countries tax individuals on their *worldwide income*. On obtaining Spanish residence, for example, you would become liable to Spanish income tax on your worldwide income. With Spanish tax rates of up to 48%, avoiding UK tax is not as big a benefit as it seems!

However, not all countries tax residents on their worldwide income. In Malta, for example, individuals who are of non-Malta domicile, and who are resident but not ordinarily resident in Malta, pay tax only on income arising in Malta, or income remitted there.

If you seek to minimise income tax, your choice of country of residence is critical. In addition, the terms of any applicable double tax treaty should be examined carefully. Double tax treaties are covered later in the book but it is worthwhile noting that you would be entitled to a 'set off' where tax was suffered in two countries on the same income.

Chapter 5

How to Avoid UK Capital Gains Tax

5.1   Introduction

In order for an individual to avoid capital gains tax it is usually necessary to remain non-resident for **five complete tax years**. Any gains on assets disposed of during the period of non-residence will then escape UK capital gains tax completely.

It should be noted that this rule only applies if you have been UK resident for at least four of the seven tax years prior to the year of your departure.

If you have not been UK resident for this time, it is still possible to avoid capital gains tax by becoming non-UK resident and non-UK ordinarily resident for the tax year of the disposal (for example, by working abroad under a full time contract of employment that spans a complete tax year). Provided you then remain non-resident for at least five complete tax years, gains realised in the first five complete tax years of non-residence are totally free of UK taxes.

If you become UK resident within the five-year period, any gains on assets disposed of during your absence from the UK will be assessed as having arisen in the tax year in which they are sold.

5.2   Countries with Generous CGT Rules

It should be noted that the above five-year rule for capital gains tax is without prejudice to double tax treaties. In other words, you may still end up paying tax. The UK has concluded tax treaties with over 100 states and most of these give the country of residence sole taxing rights over capital gains (except if the gain arises from land or assets used in a permanent establishment, eg your home).

Therefore you can avoid *UK capital gains tax* if you move to a country with which the UK has concluded an appropriate double tax treaty. But you may still end up paying tax on your capital gains in the new country.

The key here is to find a treaty country that does not tax capital gains or has a favourable capital gains tax regime. For example, some countries such as South Africa will rebase the cost of your assets to their current market value and only tax you on gains generated thereafter.

The tax saving potential of this 'immigration at market value' rule should not be underestimated. Essentially it wipes out any existing gain on the asset for tax purposes. Capital gains are generally calculated by subtracting cost from selling price. So the higher the cost (by rebasing to current market value) the lower the capital gain and hence the lower your tax bill.

Example 1

Gerard, a UK resident individual, has built a big investment property portfolio in the UK. The estimated gain after all available reliefs is £800,000. This will result in capital gains tax of about £320,000. If Gerard emigrates to a country with the immigration at market value rule, the cost of the assets would now be their market value. Assuming he plans to stay in this country for at least five complete UK tax years, any sale would not be subject to UK capital gains tax. Any taxation charge in the country of residence would be minimal assuming property prices have not increased rapidly since emigrating. Gerard could therefore save significant amounts of capital gains tax, although the personal upheaval may outweigh the tax benefits.

Other countries also offer attractive tax benefits that are worth considering.

The Tax legislation in Canada allows an immigrant to shelter non-Canadian income and capital gains for up to five years after arriving in the country. The sixty-month period commences on January 1 of the calendar year during which the taxpayer becomes resident in Canada for tax purposes. Maximum benefit can be made of this tax break by transferring income producing assets that are situated outside Canada into an offshore trust.

All income and capital gains earned by these assets escape Canadian tax during the five-year period. If the trust continues in place thereafter and the person remains resident in Canada for tax purposes, the trust itself will become a resident taxpayer and liable for Canadian taxation on its worldwide income. This would therefore allow non-Canadian assets to be protected from Canadian tax for a period of at least five years on taking up Canadian residence. A decision could then be made as to whether Canadian residence was to be continued, the assets to be sold, or the trust structure is to be dissolved.

However, if the taxpayer obtains Canadian citizenship within the five-year period and then emigrates from Canada, the income and capital gains produced by the offshore trust will be completely free of Canadian tax.

The advantage of using the offshore trust to hold the non-Canadian assets is that if you decided to remain resident in Canada as a Canadian resident and citizen beyond the five-year period, you could re-acquire the assets from the offshore trust at their current market value – for appreciating assets this would ensure a tax-free uplift in the base cost!

International Capital Gains Tax Rates

To give you an idea of how other countries tax capital gains, the table below shows a selection of countries and the CGT rates that would generally apply to gains on assets that have been held for at least 12 months.

International Capital Gains Tax Rates

	%
Australia	48.5
Belgium	0
Canada	23.5
China	20
France	26
Germany	0
Hong Kong	0
Italy	12.5 or 27
Japan	20
Mexico	0
Netherlands	0
Poland	0
Singapore	0
Sweden	30
United States	15

However, these are only a simple guide. Taking Australia for instance, one method to reduce this rate would be to hold on to any asset for at least 12 months. If you do, you would only have to pay capital gains tax on half the gain you've made, which gives a taxpayer paying tax at the top tax rate an effective CGT rate of 24.25 per cent. There are also often separate rates for gains on property, shares or other assets.

In addition, these rates only apply to capital gains tax rates. Some countries, such as Belgium do not have capital gains tax. However, certain gains are taxed as income.

Therefore, as always there is no substitute for obtaining good, up-to-date professional advice.

5.3   Exceptions to the Five-year Rule

There are a few exceptions to the 'five-year rule' that should be borne in mind:

1. It only applies to individuals who go overseas after 17 March 1998. For those who were non-resident prior to this date it is only necessary that they are non-UK resident during the tax year the asset is sold in order for any gains to be tax free. Of course, in practical terms this rule was of most importance in the past, as most individuals who were non-resident on 17 March 1998, would now have been non-resident for five tax years – in other words their gains will be tax free.

2. The rule only applies to assets held by the emigrant at the date of departure from the UK. Assets purchased during a tax year of non-residence, are not subject to UK capital gains tax, provided you are also non-resident during the tax year they are sold. The requirement for five complete years of non-residence does not come into play in these circumstances.

Example

Peter left the UK in May 2001 and has not returned to the UK since this date. He bought a UK property in September 2002. The Inland Revenue accepted that Peter has been non-resident and not ordinarily resident since the date of his departure. If the property is sold in the 2003/2004 tax year it would be exempt from UK capital gains tax, as the property was both acquired and disposed of whilst Peter was a non-resident. Even if he was to subsequently become UK resident in the 2004/2005 tax year, the gain would not be taxable.

Therefore those thinking about investing in property prior to moving overseas would be better off delaying the acquisition until after the move overseas. Provided you sell the property while you are still non-resident, you will pay no tax even if you become UK resident before the expiration of the five-year period.

3. UK tax legislation is generally subject to the terms of any relevant double tax treaty. Therefore, if you can become resident in a country that excludes the five-year requirement, you would only need to be non-resident during the tax year the asset is sold.

5.4 Belgium

Belgium is traditionally seen as a favoured jurisdiction because it allows the five-year rule to be avoided on disposals of some UK assets. Under the UK/Belgium double tax treaty capital gains are taxed only in the country of residence. Therefore, if you were to become resident in Belgium, any gain arising during the non-resident period will be exempt from UK tax even if you return to the UK within five years. In addition, under the Belgian tax rules there will not usually be any tax to pay as the country has no capital gains tax.

It is worth bearing in mind that although there is no general capital gains tax in Belgium, gains that are 'speculative' are likely to be taxed at 33% and the sale of certain assets including the sale of Belgian property will attract a charge to tax in some circumstances.

Significantly, the benefits under the treaty do not apply to gains made in respect of UK 'real' property (essentially land and property).

Given this, individuals with significant inbuilt gains on shares often choose Belgium as their 'home' for a number of years.

When considering taking advantage of the treaty, there are a number of points that should be borne in mind. Care needs to be taken to ensure that the taxpayer actually becomes resident in Belgium for the purposes of the treaty.

Meeting the criteria would in all likelihood involve the purchase of a property in Belgium and the sale of any available UK home.

Also, to be more likely of achieving non-resident status for the purposes of the treaty, it would be advisable to be resident in Belgium for at least two years.

A 'tightening up' of the double taxation treaty between the UK and Belgium has been proposed that will put an end to the current capital gains tax benefit opportunities.

However, this has not yet been done and there is no fixed timetable to do so.

5.5 Traps to Avoid in the Year You Depart

Gains accruing on a disposal of assets in the tax year of departure are subject to capital gains tax *even though the disposal may only occur after you have left the UK*. This is an important trap to avoid.

Example
Paul left the UK on 17 November 2004. It is his intention to remain overseas permanently. He is therefore likely to be given split year treatment and treated as non-resident from 18 November 2004 onwards. He owns a property that has previously been rented out and is keen to dispose of it as soon as possible.

A disposal prior to 5 April 2005 would result in him paying capital gains tax for tax year 2004/2005.

If Paul were to dispose of the property after 6 April 2005 (in other words, at the beginning of the next tax year) the gain would arise in a tax year that he was non-resident. Provided he stays non-resident until on or after 6 April 2010, any gain will be completely free of UK capital gains tax.

If Paul were to become UK resident in tax year 2006/2007 Inland Revenue will claim the right to tax him and the gain will be treated as having arisen in the 2006/07 tax year.

5.6 Out of the Frying Pan and into the Fire

You need to always look at the overseas tax regime, and how it will apply to both your future income and assets, and your current assets, held at the date of emigration.

We've already looked at situations where assets should be sold after departure to take advantage of the capital gains tax exemption for non-residents, and any uplift in cost to market value.

What about the reverse scenario? It should not always be assumed that UK capital gains tax will be higher than that of the other country.

In fact there are a number of situations where disposing of assets whilst UK resident would reduce the overall tax charge, including:

- Where a CGT exemption exists such as principal private residence relief (PPR). A disposal whilst UK resident would ensure there was no chargeable gain. However, leaving the disposal until you become non-UK resident could substantially increase the tax charge if the new country of residence is not as favourable.

  Whilst many countries operate a form of PPR relief, few will deem the last 36 months of ownership as exempt for CGT purposes!

- Where UK reliefs significantly reduce any gain. The key example here would be business asset taper relief. This can potentially eliminate 75% of any gain, resulting in a tax rate for a higher rate taxpayer of 10%.

  We've already mentioned the use of Belgium, but if proper tax planning advice was not followed and, for example, shares were disposed of and caught by the 33% Belgian tax charge, the taxpayer would be much worse off than a disposal whilst UK resident.

- Where the overseas country taxes gains at a much higher rate than the UK. Although the UK rate of 40% seems high, when other reliefs such as the annual exemption and taper relief are taken into account, it may well be the case that many emigrants (to Spain, for example) could end up paying more in CGT than a disposal whilst UK resident.

5.7 How to Postpone Disposals and Avoid Paying Capital Gains Tax

An emigrant avoids capital gains tax if a disposal is delayed until the tax year following departure.

Therefore if Paul in the above example needed to postpone the disposal until 2005/2006, *no contract should be entered into until after 6 April 2005.*

One key trap to watch out for is, with the exception of land, Inland Revenue may contend that there has been an oral contract for disposal prior to emigration. The emigrant should ensure that this possibility is considered and that no evidence is available to support this contention.

There are usually two possible methods of postponing a disposal: using conditional contracts and using options.

Conditional contracts

A disposal under a conditional contract only occurs when the condition is satisfied. A contract is only conditional if :

- The condition is satisfied prior to the contract being 'completed', and
- It is within neither parties' direct power to bring it about.

A good example of a conditional contract is a contract that is subject to a third party consent, eg the granting of planning permission.

Options

Options can be either call options, whereby the purchaser is entitled to call on the vendor to sell the asset, or put options in terms of which the vendor can require the purchaser to buy the asset. Options can therefore be used to delay the actual contract date, as the contract is not concluded until the option is satisfied.

5.8 Avoiding Capital Gains Tax on Business Assets

There is one key exception to the general rule that emigration takes UK assets out of the UK capital gains tax net, namely where a 'branch or agency trade' exists.

A branch or agency trade can exist when any business is being run from the UK. Therefore someone who leaves the country and retains a business and appoints a manager to run it, may find that a branch or agency trade exists.

In addition, a branch/agency trade exists if the emigrant is a partner in a UK partnership with capital gains apportioned between the partners. In this case, gains on UK assets are subject to UK capital gains tax if they are used by either the branch or trade.

A problem therefore arises where an individual operates via an unincorporated business (eg, a sole trader business or partnership). Once the proprietor leaves the country, the business will usually become a branch or agency trade and gains on the business assets will accordingly remain subject to capital gains tax.

There are two common ways around this difficulty:

- Sell the business before you emigrate and reinvest the proceeds in the assets of a new business situated abroad. In these circumstances, roll over relief is available and the gain arising on the business assets can be effectively rolled over and, as the emigrant remains non-resident, the gain is completely sheltered.

- Transfer the business to a company prior to leaving the country. If the transfer includes all the assets of the business, the business is a trading business and shares in the company are the sole consideration received by the individual, then the capital gain is rolled over against the cost of the company shares. As the shares are not a business, there will be no branch/agency capital gains tax charge when you sell the shares.

Care must, however, be taken with the latter method, particularly given the large number of cases coming before the courts regarding anti avoidance. To avoid attack under anti avoidance principles, the transfer to the company should take place *before* the sale is negotiated.

5.9 Sale of a Former Home

An individual leaving the UK may decide to not dispose of their UK home until after they have left the UK. It should be remembered that there is no UK capital gains tax on the sale of a main residence. As a result, sale of such a property whilst an individual is UK resident is still a good option.

On becoming resident in another country, care must be taken as regards the tax liability in the new country of residence, as many countries charge residents capital gains tax on their worldwide disposals. In such a case, it is necessary to identify whether the UK has a double tax treaty with the country in question. Under the terms of many double tax treaties, 'immovable property' can be taxed in the country where the property is located (in other words, the UK). There would therefore be no liability to overseas taxation (as the property is UK situated) and no UK liability would arise providing you satisfied the five-year test (in other words, you did not become UK resident within five tax years of the date of departure).

Example

Catriana, emigrated to Spain during the 2004/2005 tax year. She has purchased a property in Spain, and has become a Spanish resident. She still owns a UK property, which has increased in value significantly. She has decided to sell the UK property, and needs to know whether there will be any UK or Spanish tax on a disposal of the property under the terms of Article 13(1) of the UK-Spain double tax treaty (see Appendix 1), the capital gain arising on the sale of the property can be liable to tax in the country where the property is situated. This is further developed by Article 24(4), which provides that the property will be treated as a UK source, and therefore liable to UK tax.

Since an individual who is neither resident or ordinarily resident in the UK is exempt from UK capital gains tax (unless the assets are used in connection with a UK trade), the disposal would escape tax altogether.

5.10 Favourable Tax Jurisdictions

There are a number of countries that offer favourable tax regimes. Given the complexities involved, and the differing approaches taken by other tax authorities, it is essential that you obtain detailed and specific advice from a suitably qualified tax specialist in the relevant country.

In addition, tax should not be your main consideration when considering a move abroad. Other factors that you would probably consider are political and economic stability, domestic crime levels, access to quality healthcare, climate, distance from the UK/family, telecommunications, the banking system and ease of obtaining residence.

One of the biggest dangers facing those who move abroad but retain significant UK assets and income is currency movements. The Euro, for example, has gyrated wildly against the Pound since its launch and other currencies behave even more erratically. This can play havoc with your personal financial planning.

It's also critical to avoid substituting a lower tax bill for other financial burdens, such as expensive property and high living costs in your new country of residence.

Some of the countries that offer favourable tax regimes include:

The Cayman Islands

The Cayman Islands impose no taxes other than import duties and stamp duty. In addition, they have no double tax treaties.

Andorra

There are no taxes in Andorra. The only things you have to watch out for are rates and some property transaction taxes. There is no double tax treaty with the UK.

Gibraltar

The main benefit of Gibraltar is that there is no capital gains tax or VAT. Income tax is, however, payable. Individuals pay quite high taxes on their income in Gibraltar unless they can take advantage of 'High Net Worth Individual' status, which is granted to certain wealthy individuals. Income tax is payable at rates of between 17% and 45%.

Cyprus

Cyprus charges both income tax and capital gains tax, although capital gains tax does not apply to profits from the sale of overseas property by non-residents, or by residents who were not resident when they purchased the asset. The capital gains tax rate is 20%.

Malta

Individuals who are domiciled and ordinarily resident in Malta pay income tax on their worldwide income. Individuals who are domiciled elsewhere, and who are resident but not ordinarily resident in Malta pay tax on their income arising in Malta, or remitted there, but not on capital gains.

Monaco

Monaco levies no personal taxes, although there are inheritance and gift taxes, along with business profits tax. VAT is also charged on goods and services.

5.11 Using Enterprise Investment Schemes & Venture Capital Trusts

An important point to note is that any relief given to an individual on shares acquired by him (or in certain circumstances his spouse) may be clawed back if the individual ceases to be resident or ordinarily resident in the UK. Therefore any gains deferred under the Enterprise Investment Scheme or the Venture Capital Trust scheme will be brought back into the tax net. This does not apply if you go abroad for less than three years in the course of a full time job (note that gains will not be able to be deferred using VCTs following the 2004 Budget).

Example
Jack sold his investment company at a gain of £500,000. He reinvested £500,000 of the proceeds in qualifying EIS shares in order to defer the gain on the investment company. He has purchased a property in Majorca and intends to regularly holiday in Spain. Jack needs to be very careful that he does not become

non UK resident. If he was to fall outside the residency limits examined earlier there would be a considerable problem:

- *He will be non resident, so still liable to UK income tax on any UK source income.*
- *He has no overseas income and so will not benefit from the exempton from UK income tax on overseas income.*
- *He will still be ordinarily resident and within the scope of UK capital gains tax.*
- *He will still be UK domiciled and therefore within the scope of UK inheritance tax.*
- *He will have a 'deemed gain' in relation to the gain held over in the tax year of departure (£500,000). Given that his cash is tied up in the shares and there has been no actual disposal, this could cause severe cash flow problems.*

5.12 Offshore Investments for UK Residents

What about the typical British person who is both UK resident and UK domiciled - are there any offshore techniques they can use to minimise UK tax?

The first point to bear in mind is that, as a UK resident, you will be taxed on your worldwide income and gains under domestic tax legislation. Therefore, the scope to generate returns in a more tax efficient manner is limited.

Example
Herbert a UK resident and domiciled individual wants to invest in overseas equities. He decides to invest purely through an offshore broker, and will invest in shares quoted on the US stock market. He will be fully liable to UK capital gains tax on his profits.

However, there are specific exceptions contained within the tax legislation that apply to offshore bonds.

Offshore Bonds

Qualifying offshore bonds allow investors to 'roll up' their returns – this means tax is only paid at the end of the investment period (usually five to 10 years) when the investment is cashed in.

A withdrawal of up to 5% can be taken each year, with tax only payable at the end of the investment period. If you exceed the 5% limit a tax liability is triggered.

It is also possible to switch in and out of different investment funds within an offshore bond wrapper, without these transfers being classified as chargeable events for capital gains tax purposes.

Investment in these qualifying offshore bonds can prove highly tax effective. Investments grow virtually tax free within the fund, benefiting from what is known as 'gross roll up'. This means that, rather than an investment being taxed on an ongoing basis, the funds grow without the encumbrance of tax.

Whilst there may be personal tax to pay when the investment is cashed in, proper tax planning, such as arranging your affairs so that you are non UK resident at the date of encashment, can help reduce this.

Gross roll up can lead to dramatic increase in the amount of money invested.

For example, an individual investing £50,000 in a bond, assuming a 7% growth rate would have the following amounts at the end of a 20 year period:

Onshore bond	£145,000
Offshore bond (taxed on encashment at 22%)	£161,000
Offshore bond - no income tax	£192,000

Therefore the offshore bond could accumulate approximately £47,000 of additional capital which could be used for retirement.

Capital gains tax is not levied within the fund on offshore bonds, so an investment may be actively managed focusing solely on the investment considerations rather than being subject, as in the UK, to capital gains tax within the fund.

Savings can often be made with offshore bonds since investors can buy and sell qualifying investments held within the bond without any liability to capital gains tax. Many offshore bond providers offer links to third-party, household name, investment companies, so finding a suitable investment shouldn't be difficult.

However, on the back of the 2004 budget, the Inland Revenue have announced changes that will affect when offshore investment bonds will be able to benefit from the income tax and gross roll up treatment described above.

These changes are pretty technical, and as such it would be advisable to seek confirmation from any potential fund provider whether the chosen fund falls within the above tax rules.

If the fund does not qualify for the gross roll up, the investment would be treated just as any other UK investment. This would eliminate the UK tax benefit as purchases and disposals of the investments or units within the bond would be subject to UK capital gains tax.

Chapter 6

How to Avoid Inheritance Tax

6.1   Introduction

The general rule is that an individual domiciled in the UK will be subject to inheritance tax on his or her *worldwide assets*. Non UK domiciled individuals are only subject to UK inheritance tax on their *UK assets*.

In order to lose your UK domicile you will need to build up evidence to show that you have abandoned your UK domicile of origin and have acquired a new domicile of choice.

This is something that many who leave the country do not do... with disastrous tax consequences. Frequently they return to the UK on many occasions, keeping within the 90 days a year *income tax* limit. This pattern of behaviour is likely to indicate that you have not abandoned your domicile of origin, with the result that you will be subject to UK inheritance tax on your worldwide assets.

In order to safeguard your overseas estate from inheritance tax, you are likely to have to make some significant changes to your lifestyle in order to produce evidence that you have a new domicile of choice.

6.2   How to Lose Your UK Domicile

You should take as many of the following steps as possible in order to show evidence of an intention to acquire a new domicile of choice:

- Take up nationality in the new country.
- Join clubs and other social organisations in the new country.
- Dispose of UK investments.
- Resign from clubs in the UK.
- Close UK bank accounts.
- Avoid subscriptions to British newspapers.
- Dispose of all UK private residences.
- Buy a new residence in the new country.
- Make a will under the laws of the new country.
- Build up a new circle of friends in the new country.
- Avoid retaining directorships in the UK.
- Exercise any vote in the new country.

It should be noted that none of the above factors are in themselves conclusive. However, Inland Revenue will look at all the factors that can be put in evidence to determine whether there is a settled intention to reside permanently in the new country.

Obtaining a non-UK domicile of choice does not protect you completely from UK inheritance tax. You will still be liable to tax on your UK assets. If the value of these assets is less than the the nil rate band (currently £263,000 for tax year 2004/2005) it is probably not worth taking any further action, unless you expect your assets to rise significantly in value.

If you wish to keep significant UK assets, one option would be to place an overseas company between yourself and your assets. What you would then own are shares in an overseas company – a *non* UK asset. Care must, however, be taken with the disposal, to ensure that any gain falls outside of the scope of UK capital gains tax. The use of offshore companies is explained in detail later on.

6.3   How to Establish an Overseas Domicile

In practical terms it is difficult for UK emigrants to convince the UK taxman that they have a non UK domicile.

A form, 'DOM 1', is available from Inland Revenue which can be used where an individual considers they are non UK domiciled. However, it is only necessary for the Inland Revenue to consider your domicile if it is immediately relevant in deciding your UK income tax and/or capital gains tax liability. If you are non resident, this will not be an issue, as you will not in any event be subject to UK capital gains tax or income tax on overseas capital gains and income.

Therefore, by ticking the non domicile box in your tax return, or completing form DOM 1, the Inland Revenue is unlikely to enter into correspondence with you regarding your tax status, as your domicile will have no impact on your immediate UK income tax or capital gains tax liability. For a non resident, the only impact of non domicile status is for UK inheritance tax.

It cannot be assumed that you are of non UK domicile if the Inland Revenue does not look into the issue during your lifetime. If you wish to determine your domicile position prior to death, there are methods available.

One method would be to gift cash or assets (above the £263,000 nil rate band) to a discretionary trust or company. Provided the cash or assets are situated overseas, inheritance tax would be payable unless you have lost your UK domicile. Accordingly, if the taxman does not try and make you pay IHT it will be clear that he accepts that you have acquired a foreign domicile.

6.4 Retaining Your Domicile of Origin

Many UK immigrants and their children are non UK domiciled. There are substantial tax advantages to be had from retaining this status: In particular:

- Overseas assets can be passed though the family free from UK inheritance tax.

- Overseas assets can be used to generate income offshore. Provided the income is not brought into the UK, there will be no liability to UK taxation.

- There are greater opportunities to use offshore trusts and companies, as many of the anti-avoidance rules apply only to UK domiciliaries.

Great, you're thinking, I like the sound of that. As always however, you and your offspring need to be careful:

Firstly, the deemed domicile rules (Chapter 2) will deem you to be UK domiciled for IHT purposes, after you've been here for 17 years. Many families will find that their children are subject to UK IHT as a result of this rule. Note, however, that the deemed domicile only applies for inheritance tax purposes. Your children could still accumulate assets offshore without paying any UK tax.

The next risk is that the taxman may contend that you or your children have acquired a UK domicile of choice. This is very likely if you have stayed in the UK for a number of years. To establish that you have acquired a UK domicile of choice, the evidence would need to point to the fact that you intend to stay in the UK permanently.

There are a number of other options that could be considered to minimize UK inheritance tax. These are considered elsewhere in the book, however they include:

- Using mortgages/loans to reduce the value of your estate.

- Using an offshore structure to avoid estate taxes.

- For non domiciliaries, disposing of UK assets and purchasing assets overseas. The capital gains tax implications (both UK and overseas) should be considered, however, for an individual who intends to remain overseas for a significant period, UK CGT would not be an issue, and dependent on the terms of any double tax treaty and domestic tax legislation, there may not in fact be any overseas tax charged.

- Investment in assets that qualify for Business Property Relief ('BPR'), eg shares in unquoted trading companies and assets used in a trading business.

Chapter 7

How Foreign Nationals Can Escape UK Tax

7.1 Non UK Domiciliaries

Individuals who are UK resident/ordinarily resident but retain a foreign domicile enjoy preferential tax treatment in a number of respects.

The type of person who can exploit these tax breaks is typically someone who was born outside the UK but currently lives here. Their children are usually also able to take advantage of these tax planning opportunities.

The main tax benefit is that overseas income and capital gains are only subject to income tax and capital gains tax on the 'remittance basis'. This means that tax is paid only when the funds are brought into the UK. This is a fantastic tax break because it means that your investments can grow tax free for many years and potentially indefinitely.

Inheritance tax, being based on domicile, would not normally apply. However, the deemed domicile rules for inheritance tax purposes will result in your worldwide estate being subject to inheritance tax if you are UK resident for 17 out of the last 20 years.

7.2 Income Tax Planning

A foreign domiciliary is subject to income tax on a remittance basis in respect of income arising from foreign securities and overseas possessions. For this purpose a trade carried on outside the UK is regarded as an overseas possession.

But what about salary?

Foreign emoluments/salary

These were considered earlier, however it is useful to explain the rule again. There is a separate rule for certain foreign emoluments (emoluments in this context can be taken to mean salary). A foreign domiciliary who is resident in the UK is taxed on a remittance basis only on any emoluments which are paid to him (a) by a non UK resident employer and (b) in respect of an office or employment the duties of which are only performed abroad.

If your work duties are not performed abroad only, then the income is taxed as and when it arises.

7.3 Using Split Contracts to Reduce Income Tax

It is not uncommon for foreign domiciliaries working in the UK to have two separate employments. One will cover the UK duties and the other will cover the overseas duties.

The benefit of this arrangement is that the overseas duties will only be subject to UK tax on the remittance basis (in other words, under Schedule E, Case III as mentioned earlier).

Clearly legal advice should be taken as to the precise provisions of the employment contracts, however it is worthwhile noting that care should be taken to ensure that a degree of 'commerciality' is retained.

Each contract should be reasonable (eg, the level of remuneration should be closely related to the duties to be performed) and should clearly lay out the employment duties. If possible, separate employers/companies should be used, so that the employment does not appear to have been artificially separated.

Example
Richard a non-UK domiciliary has been offered full time employment with his UK employer's Rome office. The duties of the employment will be split approximately 40% (UK), 60% (Rome).

On this basis, all of the income (assuming Richard is UK resident) would be subject to UK income tax under Schedule E, Case I. Schedule E, Case III (remittance basis) would not apply as the employment duties are not only performed abroad.

If separate contracts were used for the UK and Rome employment duties, then the UK employment would be subject to UK income tax, whereas the Rome employment would fall under the remittance basis of Schedule E, Case III.

7.4 Capital Gains Tax Planning

As stated above, capital gains in respect of assets situated outside of the UK are taxable on the remittance basis. Any capital losses are not allowable.

Example
Steve, a non UK domiciliary has been living in the UK for 8 years and is therefore classed as UK resident. He has overseas assets that originally cost him £100,000 and he is planning to sell them for £150,000.

The gain of £50,000 (less any reliefs) will not be subject to UK capital gains tax - provided the proceeds of £150,000 are not brought into the country, for example, deposited in a UK bank account or used to settle UK debts.

If only part of the proceeds is remitted, then only part of the gain is taxable. For example, if £15,000 of proceeds is remitted to the UK, £5,000 would be taxable. (Note how the proportions are what matter. £5000 is to £15,000 what £50,000 is to £150,000.) One way of using the remittance basis to avoid paying tax is to remit just enough of the proceeds to make use of your annual capital gains tax allowance.

So if proceeds of £24,600 were remitted in the 2004/05 tax year, the taxable gain would be £8,200. As the annual exemption is £8,200 the gain would be completely tax free.

7.5 Making the Most of the Remittance Rules

It is often advisable for foreign domiciliaries to have at least three overseas bank accounts:

- The first account for your existing capital.

- The second account to deposit the proceeds of any asset disposals.

- The third account to contain the interest from the first two accounts, along with any other foreign source income.

The point of this exercise is to segregate your foreign income and gains.

If you want to bring money into the country you should first remit funds from the first bank account. This can usually be done tax free. If further funds are required, then withdrawals can be made from the second account, which would effectively subject the withdrawals to capital gains tax. However, it is possible these amounts will be tax free if they are covered by the annual exemption of £8,200. Finally, withdrawals from the third account would be subject to income tax.

Another advantage of utilising these accounts is that, for inheritance tax purposes, the foreign bank accounts of a non UK domiciliary will usually be outside the scope of UK inheritance tax.

Example

Hercule, who was born in Belgium, has been offered a contract of employment with a UK company. It is envisaged that he will be in the UK for five years before returning to Belgium.

Hercule has significant assets in France and has decided to dispose of his main residence before he commences his UK employment. Any proceeds of this sale should be put into overseas account 1. One year after the commencement of his contract, he hears that the Belgium property market is about to collapse and he decides to sell his other Belgian property. The proceeds of this sale should go into overseas account 2. Any overseas income that he earns, for example rental income from his properties or interest on his overseas bank accounts should be deposited in overseas account 3.

Hercule may never need to use any of his foreign income/proceeds during his period of stay in the UK, in which case none of the foreign income/gains would be taxable. If he does require any funds they should be remitted in the following order:

- **Account 1** - *Not subject to UK capital gains tax as the assets were disposed of before Hercule was UK resident.*
- **Account 2** - *Subject to UK capital gains tax on a remittance basis, as the disposal occurred while Hercule was UK resident but non domiciled. Capital gains tax is usually preferable to income tax as there are more reliefs available.*
- **Account 3** - *Subject to UK income tax on the remittance basis as overseas income of a UK resident/non domiciliary.*

7.6 Paying Less Tax on Investment Income

As UK resident non domiciliaries are only subject to tax on the remittance basis it is often suggested that they should transfer their UK savings offshore and avoid UK income tax.

This is certainly possible. However, it is also clearly beneficial to keep existing overseas assets such as property and bank accounts and avoid bringing the money into the UK in the first place. This then avoids an extra 'layer' of UK tax.

Any cash saved by a UK resident will have already been subject to UK income tax, either as salary or business income. Transferring the cash into an overseas account does not result in any UK tax charge and any interest earned would be overseas income. This would be subject to UK income tax only if it is brought into the UK. If funds were required it would be beneficial to remit part of the cash deposited abroad as this is not overseas income, merely cash earned in the UK and credited to an overseas account.

This is easier to manage if a separate account is set up into which the interest is paid. It would then be clear that the cash remitted to the UK was not the overseas interest income.

Finally, it is important to note that the concept of 'remittance' can have a wide meaning. For example, using a UK credit card and clearing the balance with overseas income would constitute a remittance to the UK.

7.7 Incorporating Your Business to Avoid Capital Gains Tax

We have already mentioned that one of the options open to a possible emigrant who owns a UK business is to incorporate the business and dispose of the shares whilst non resident. Suppose the individual is of non UK domicile and cannot become non resident at the date of disposal and for 5 complete tax years.

Could he incorporate his business (using an overseas company) and then have any disposal taxed on the remittance basis?
This question is best answered by means of an example:

Example

John is of French domicile, yet has been resident in the UK for 5 years. During this period he has built up a successful publishing business. He now wishes to retire to France and is interested in minimising his UK tax liabilities.

In theory, it would be possible for John to transfer his business to a non resident company (with no immediate capital gains tax charge). He would have then converted a UK asset (in other words, the trade & assets) to an overseas asset (the company shares). Any subsequent gain on disposal of the shares would be assessed on a remittance basis, and providing the proceeds were retained overseas, there would be no liability to pay UK capital gains tax.

Any individual considering such a course of action would be well advised to take professional advice. Whilst in principle there is nothing technically wrong with such structuring, the taxman can and has successfully challenged this, particularly where there has been no commercial motive for transferring the trade to an overseas company, and where the transfer was made in anticipation of a sale.

7.8 Buying Property Overseas

For those who are UK resident and ordinarily resident but non UK domiciled, purchasing overseas property can offer a number of attractive tax breaks. For income tax and capital gains tax purposes the remittance basis applies. This means that any rental income obtained from the overseas property will be exempt from UK tax provided the income is not remitted to the UK.

In addition when the property is eventually sold no UK capital gains tax will be payable unless the funds are brought into the country.

However, the benefit of the remittance basis is for many more apparent than real. Overseas tax is likely to be payable, unless the property is purchased in a country that does not levy any. Most double tax treaties state that immovable property is taxed in the country in which it is located (in other words the overseas jurisdiction). Therefore it is overseas tax that will have the biggest impact. And the traditional European countries most individuals choose to invest in have high tax rates.

For example, in Spain sales of property by non-Spanish residents are taxed at 35%. The gain is calculated as the difference between the sales price and the original purchase price, including any investment made or improvement work carried out. There is also an adjustment to take account of inflation. In addition, the purchaser must retain 5% of the price and pay this as tax on behalf of the non-resident.

The non UK domiciled and UK resident investing in Spain will also need to pay any local taxes relating to the property, as well as other domestic taxes. For example, Spain has a wealth tax, which would tax the value of a non resident's Spanish assets above a certain amount.

In Italy, capital gains realized on the sale of property are subject to personal income tax. This tax is calculated on the taxpayer's total income. A progressive rate is used and the tax is settled by means of an annual income statement. The rate can be as high as 45%.

The gain is calculated as the difference between the amount received and the original purchase cost of the property. Capital gains realized on the sale of building land are also subject to income tax, irrespective of the period of ownership.

There are exemptions, for example, gains arising on the sale of inherited property or your main residence are not subject to Italian tax.

In France, as a non-resident, the UK resident non domiciliary pays capital gains tax on the gain arising on the disposal of French property. This is usually deducted from the sale proceeds by the 'Notaire' who pays it over to the local tax authorities. At present, capital gains tax is payable at 33.3% by all non-French residents.

It is possible to deduct costs such as original purchase costs (notaire's fee, estate agent's fee), cost of renovation work (but not simple re-decorating costs), mortgage interest etc, providing that these haven't also been offset against any rental income. In addition, it is possible to make an allowance for inflation, calculated by application of a table in accordance with the year of purchase of the property.

The amount of the taxable gain is then subject to tapered relief if it has been owned for more than two years. For each year that the property has been held beyond this initial two year period, the gain is reduced by 5% (for ten years of ownership, the reduction is thus 40%). Therefore, if a property has been owned for more than 22 years, the relief is 100% and no capital gains tax is payable.

Just as in the UK, there are a number of exclusions and exemptions, and if you are considering purchasing a property in any overseas jurisdiction, it is essential to obtain tax advice from a tax specialist in the country in question.

The only sure fire way for the non domiciliary to avoid taxes altogether is to purchase overseas property in a country that levies no capital gains tax, eg the Isle of Man. It would therefore only be if a property was purchased in a 'tax haven' that tax could be avoided.

Inheritance Tax

Again, from a UK tax perspective, there would be no UK IHT impact. As a non UK domiciliary, your taxable estate would include only include your UK assets. However, overseas tax would be payable, unless the property was located in a country that did not levy inheritance tax.

Use of Trusts

As a non UK domiciliary, an offshore trust could be created. For IHT purposes, the trust would not be subject to UK IHT as the assets of the trust would be overseas assets.

From a capital gains tax perspective, the trustees would not be liable to UK capital gains tax, as the trust would be non resident. Providing the settlor retains his non UK domicile status, the UK anti-avoidance provisions attributing/deeming gains would not apply.

Providing the overseas jurisdiction did not levy capital gains tax, there would also be no overseas tax charge (eg the Isle of Man).

Chapter 8

Working Overseas - a Powerful Tax Shelter

8.1 Introduction

If you go abroad under a full-time contract of employment you will usually be regarded as non resident and not ordinarily resident from the date of departure if:

- All your work duties are performed overseas, or any duties performed in the UK are incidental to the overseas employment, and
- Your absence from the UK is for a period which includes a complete tax year, and
- Visits to the UK do not exceed six months or more in a tax year, or three months or more on average over the period of absence, subject to a maximum of 4 years.

This status will apply from the day following your departure until the day preceding the day you return. This rule also applies to your spouse if he or she goes abroad with you. Therefore, provided one spouse works overseas and satisfies the above requirements, the accompanying spouse will also be regarded as non resident and not ordinarily resident from the date of departure.

This means any UK income will be liable to UK income tax, whereas the overseas income will be completely exempt. From a capital gains tax perspective the scope of the rules has been widened. There will be no UK capital gains tax on either UK or overseas assets owned at the date of departure, providing you are non resident during the tax year of disposal and you remain overseas for a period of 5 complete tax years. Note that this 5 year rule does not apply to assets purchased after you become non UK resident - you would be exempt from UK capital gains tax even if they were UK assets.

Example
John is a UK resident and domiciled individual who works for a UK company. He has been offered a 12 months overseas secondment to work full time for the company's Ruritanian subsidiary company. The secondment is to commence on 1 November 2004 and John will return to the UK on 30 October 2005. Any problems?

The key problem here is that whilst John may satisfy the other requirements relating to working overseas, his absence from the UK does not span a complete *tax* year. This would therefore result in John being UK resident for the entire tax year and his overseas income being subject to UK income tax.

8.2 Tax Deductible Expenses

Where an employee is resident and ordinarily resident in the UK and performs all work duties abroad, the cost of travelling abroad to take up the employment and returning to the UK on its termination is allowable as a tax deduction.

If travel is only partly for the above purpose, relief is restricted to the relevant part.

Where the overseas duties necessitate the expense of board and lodging for the employee outside the UK and this expense is met by his employer, no tax liability will arise for the employee on the payments made.

Where you have two or more jobs, the duties of one or more of which are performed totally or partly overseas, you are entitled to tax relief for the cost of travelling between the jobs where either or both places are outside the UK.

Where an employee works overseas for a continuous period of 60 days or more, the payment by the employer for a visit by the employee's spouse/children (including a return ticket) will not be taxable.

8.3 Tax Free Termination Payments

A termination payment made to an employee can be partially free of tax providing the employer had no contractual obligation to make the payment. Assuming this is satisfied, Section 401 ITEPA 2003 will usually apply, and the first £30,000 of the termination payment will be tax free.

However where an employee has substantial foreign service it is possible to obtain additional relief and in certain circumstances to totally eliminate any UK income tax charge.

In order to totally shelter the payment from UK tax, the period of employment must include foreign service which includes:

- ¾ of the whole period of service.
- Where service has exceeded 10 years, the whole of the last 10 years.
- If more than 20 years service, ½ the period plus 10 of the last 20 years.

Where these conditions are not met the amount exempt after any other deductions (such as the £30,000 exemption) will be in the proportion of foreign service to total service. In other words a straightforward pro rata of time spent overseas to UK employment.

Example
Johnny commences employment with XYZ Plc in January 1995. He spends 2 years working at the overseas office in Germany. He is made redundant in January 2004 and is to be offered £100,000 as an ex gratia termination payment.

As Johnny's foreign service does not meet the above criteria, the amount that will be exempt will be $^2/_9$ths.

Therefore the taxable amount will be calculated as follows:

Termination payment	£100,000
Less S401 exemption	(£30,000)
	£70,000
Less foreign service relief 2/9 x £70,000	(£15,556)
Taxable receipt	£54,444

8.4 Protecting Your Property Investments from the Taxman

An individual who works abroad for a number of years may decide to keep a UK residence.

If the property is subsequently sold, will the gain be subject to UK capital gains tax?

Obviously if the individual satisfies the non residence/ordinary residence criteria at the date of disposal then any gain will be outside the scope of UK capital gains tax.

If the individual is UK resident/ordinarily resident at the date of disposal, it is necessary to look at the application of the Principal Private Residence (PPR) relief, in anticipation of returning to the UK to live in the property.

The PPR relief provides full or partial relief from capital gains tax for an individual who has occupied a property as his main residence at some point during the period of ownership.

A gain on a property will be completely exempt from capital gains tax if an individual has occupied the property as his main residence throughout his entire period of ownership.

Where an individual has occupied a property as a residence for only part of his period of ownership then a proportion of the capital gain resulting on the disposal of the property is tax free. This is calculated on the following basis:

Capital gain x Period of occupation/Period of ownership

In addition to the period that an individual actually occupies a property as his residence, when calculating the period of occupation there are certain deemed periods of occupation which are allowed to be taken into account.

Most notably, the last 36 months of ownership would always be deemed to be private occupation, irrespective of whether you actually occupied the property during this period. Please note that this relief will only apply where the property has been your main residence at some point during your ownership.

Therefore an individual does not need to reside in a property during the last 36 months of ownership in order to gain full exemption from capital gains tax on a subsequent disposal.

Example
Samantha purchased a property in December 1996 for £50,000. She lived in the property as her main residence until June 2002 when she decided to move in with her boyfriend.

The property was then left empty until June 2004 when she decided to dispose of it. Any gain on the property when disposed of in June 2004 would be fully exempt from capital gains tax.

She actually resided in the house until June 2002, and the period from June 2002 until June 2004 is covered by the last 36 months 'deemed occupation' rule.

A problem occurs if the 36 months rule does not fully cover the period when the property was not occupied (in other words, the taxable portion). What is the position then?

Fortunately, there is a special provision that relates to individuals working overseas.

Any period during which the owner worked full time in an employment wholly outside the UK, providing that both before AND after those periods it was the owner's only or main residence, is deemed private occupation.

Example

Peter purchased a house in 1996 and lived in this as his main residence until 1999. He then travelled abroad until 2001.

On his return he should ensure that he resumes occupation of the property. His period spent overseas would then not restrict the availability of the PPR exemption when he sells the property.

Chapter 9

Making the Most of Double Tax Relief

9.1 Introduction

UK residents have to pay UK tax on income from UK and overseas sources. To prevent overseas income being taxed twice - once abroad and again in the UK - relief is given in one of two ways:

- By deducting the overseas tax from the UK tax - this is known as credit relief or
- By charging to UK tax the net amount of overseas income received. In other words the amount of foreign income after foreign tax has been deducted - this is known as expense relief.

9.2 Credit Relief

The overseas income is deemed to be the top slice of income for these purposes - in other words, potentially taxed at the higher rate of 40%. If there is more than one source of foreign income, double tax relief on each source must be considered separately.

The income with the highest overseas tax is treated as the top slice of overseas income.

Credit relief is given as the lower of:

- The UK tax on the overseas income
- The overseas tax

Remember that, as complex as the rules are, the principal objective is to ensure that you do not obtain as a tax credit more than the UK rate of tax.

Therefore, if the overseas tax was charged at 50%, with UK tax being 40%, you would obtain DTR at 40%. Similarly, if the overseas tax was charged at 20%, and UK tax is 40%, you would only obtain DTR at 20%. This is best illustrated by means of an example.

Example

Doug, a UK resident individual has the following income in the 2004/2005 tax year:

Salary from UK employment	*£39,420*
UK dividends	*£1,875*
Overseas bank interest paid)	*£1,100 (50% overseas tax*

His tax calculation would be:

Salary from UK employment	*£39,240*
Overseas income	*£1,100*
UK dividends	*£1,875*
Less personal allowance	*(£4,745)*
Taxable income	*£37,470*

The income tax levied on this taxable income would be reduced by double taxation relief (DTR).

As the overseas income will be subject to tax at the higher rate (as the taxable income exceeds the higher rate band and the overseas income is regarded as the 'top slice' of income), we can calculate that the DTR will be the lower of

- *The UK tax on overseas income (40% x £1,100) = £440*
- *The overseas tax (50% x £1,100) = £550*

Therefore total DTR in this case would be £440, and this would be given as a credit against Doug's tax liability.

It should be noted that if Doug had a tax loss for the period (for example, if he were self employed and had established a trading loss for offset against his other income) then the credit relief described above would be of little use as there would be no tax liability to offset the DTR against. In such a situation, expense relief is most beneficial.

9.3 Expense Relief

As stated above, expense relief operates in a totally different way to credit relief. Instead of a credit for overseas tax, the overseas tax is simply deducted from the income before it is subject to UK tax, in other words it is a deduction from the income rather than the tax on the income.

In most circumstances, credit relief will be far more beneficial, but where an individual has no tax charge against which credit relief can operate, expense relief will be better, as it will increase the amount of the loss.

The best way to illustrate this is by means of an example.

Example

Doug's tax position for the next tax year, 2005/2006, is as follows:

Overseas income (taxed at 50%)	*£1,500*
UK trading loss	*(£10,000)*

No DTR will be given and the trading loss of £8,500 (£10,000 - £1,500) can be carried forward against future profits of the business.

Expense relief provides a better outcome. It is calculated as the net amount of overseas income, in other words £1,500 less 50% overseas tax = £750.

This increases Doug's trading loss to £9,250 (in other words, £10,000- £750).

Chapter 10

Tax Benefits of Offshore Trusts

10.1 Introduction

An offshore trust is a legal entity into which you can pass ownership and control of your assets. The assets are then managed by a trustee (such as a trusted firm of accountants or lawyers) in the interests of the beneficiaries (your family, for example). The person who puts the assets into the trust (the settlor) may have a variety of reasons for distancing himself or herself from the ownership of the assets. For example, to remain anonymous for personal or business purposes or to avoid tax.

Offshore trusts are usually set up in tax havens or low tax jurisdictions such as the Channel Islands.

10.2 How Offshore Trusts Are Taxed

A trust counts as non resident for both income tax and capital gains tax purposes if all the trustees are non resident and the general administration of the trust is carried on abroad.

As the trust is non resident it is not subject to capital gains tax in respect of UK or overseas assets (in other words, the same as an individual). Subject to anti-avoidance legislation, offshore trusts are therefore capable of sheltering both UK and foreign capital gains.

As has been mentioned earlier in relation to individuals, non residents are not subject to UK tax on foreign income and therefore in the absence of anti-avoidance legislation, offshore trusts can shelter such income. However, non residents are subject to income tax if the source of the income is in the UK (just as an individual would be). Different trusts pay tax at different rates, although the type of trust most likely to be used in offshore tax planning would be either a discretionary trust or an accumulation and maintenance trust.

These trusts would pay tax at an effective 25% on UK dividends and 40% on other income or gains.

10.3 Capital Gains Tax Consequences

The disposal of assets into a trust is a chargeable disposal for capital gains tax purposes, and therefore a capital gain would arise. As the settlor is deemed to be 'connected' with the trust, and proceeds would be deemed to be equivalent to the market value of the assets transferred, it would therefore not be possible to avoid capital gains tax by simply gifting the assets.

The most effective method of establishing a trust from a capital gains tax perspective would therefore be to invest cash, and let the trustees use this to invest as they see fit (in accordance with the trust deed). As the asset gifted is cash, it falls outside the scope of capital gains tax.

Another possibility would be to settle assets that have a low initial value but which are expected to show significant growth in value. For example, shares in a newly formed company. Any growth in the value of the shares (eg to be realised on a flotation) would occur offshore and, subject to the anti-avoidance rules, be outside the scope of UK capital gains tax.

Example
Eric is considering purchasing a share in a small South African mining company for £100,000. He is hoping that the mine will strike gold and the shares will rocket in value. Rather than purchase the shares in his own name, he goes to see his solicitor and forms an offshore trust into which he settles the £100,000. The trust then purchases the shares in the South African company. Any increase in value of the company would be effectively tax free as the trust would be outside the scope of UK capital gains tax. However, as we shall see, matters are not always that simple.

10.4 Inheritance Tax Consequences

A trust is subject to UK inheritance tax if the settlor was domiciled or deemed to be domiciled in the UK when he set up the trust.

Example
Stefano is of Italian domicile and has moved to Britain to expand his business into the UK. He has substantial assets in Italy and

wishes to protect these from inheritance tax. If Stefano sets up an offshore trust, providing he is not UK domiciled at the date of creation, the overseas assets will be outside the scope of UK inheritance tax, irrespective of the fact that Stefano may later acquire a UK domicile.

The problem with an offshore discretionary trust is that it can lead to a large inheritance tax cost for a *UK domiciled* individual (non UK domiciliaries are considered in detail below).

A transfer of assets to a discretionary trust is called a chargeable lifetime transfer (CLT). This means that a proportion of inheritance tax is paid during the settlor's lifetime.

There are a number of complex rules governing this area. However, in essence the available nil rate band remaining is deducted from the value of the gift (in other words, the assets transferred into the trust) and tax is payable at 20% or 25% depending on whether the trust or the settlor is to pay the tax.

There is also a regime for taxing the assets of the trust. This is necessary as when you transfer assets into a discretionary trust they are taken out of your estate and are therefore not subject to inheritance tax along with other assets you own.

The inheritance tax consequences of a discretionary trust are not straightforward and the calculation is pretty complex. What happens is that an effective rate of IHT is calculated based on the initial value of the trust (taking into account previous transfers and all reliefs) based on IHT payable at 6%. Then when assets are distributed out of the trust, and on every tenth anniversary of the date the trust is set up, inheritance tax is payable on the amount distributed or the trust assets. This ensures that the trust is subject to a form of inheritance tax.

In summary, there are two main circumstances where a discretionary trust is free of inheritance tax:

- Where the trust is within the settlor's nil rate band and remains within this for the following ten anniversaries.

  The key problem with this trust is that its value is limited to the amount of the nil rate band (£263,000 for tax year 2004/2005).

  One possible planning use could be to use the trust as a holding device where the value of funds initially settled is low and then perhaps distribute the funds before the trust's 10th anniversary. The benefit of this is that for an exit before the first anniversary, the rate of inheritance tax is based on the value of funds on creation. In this case there would be no inheritance tax exit charge.

- Where the assets transferred into the trust are covered by an inheritance tax exemption such as Business Property Relief ('BPR'). This relief provides for exemption from inheritance tax where 'business assets' are gifted. Typical business assets include assets used in a trade and shares in unquoted trading companies. There are a number of other conditions that would need to be satisfied to successfully claim Business Property Relief.

10.5 Dangers for UK Domiciliaries

There are two principal obstacles which UK domiciliaries have to overcome to shelter their income and gains through An offshore trust:

- Tax anti-avoidance legislation which attributes <u>income</u> to the settlor. The income of an offshore trust is assessable as the settlor's if the actual or potential beneficiaries include him or his spouse or if either of them receives a benefit.
- Anti-avoidance legislation which attributes <u>gains</u> to the settlor. The provisions attribute gains to the settlor where any 'defined persons' are actual or potential beneficiaries or receive a benefit from the trust. The term 'defined person' includes the settlor and his spouse, their children and their children's spouses and their grandchildren and their grandchildren's spouses. Clearly this is a particularly wide anti-avoidance provision.

10.6 When an Offshore Trust Can Save You Tax

There are three main situations where it is still possible for an offshore trust to operate as a tax shelter for a UK domiciled settlor:

1. Where the Settlor is Dead
Clearly the rules attributing income and gains to the settlor cannot apply if he is dead. This could arise via a trust being formed under the terms of a will.

In this case the assets would secure a tax free uplift in their base cost for capital gains tax purposes (as the assets would pass into the trust at the market value at the date of death). Of course the assets passing into the trust would be subject to any inheritance tax on death unless the value transferred falls within the nil rate band, or ther assets are covered by any other inheritance tax reliefs (such as business property relief, 'BPR').

Example

John's estate consisted of:

House	*£213,000*
Cash	*£50,000*
Shares	*£500,000*

On the assumption that the shares were in an unquoted trading company, they would qualify for Business Property Relief and the inheritance tax position would be as follows:

House	*£213,000*
Cash	*£50,000*
Nil rate band	*(£263,000)*
Shares	*£500,000*
BPR	*(£500,000)*

Therefore the inheritance tax charge would be nil.

Any subsequent gain arising on a disposal by John's heirs would be subject to UK capital gains tax (assuming the heirs are UK resident).

By contrast, John could have inserted a provision in his will for the shares to be settled in a non-resident discretionary trust. Inheritance tax would not be an issue, as the shares would qualify for BPR and, although John was a UK domiciliary, the anti avoidance provisions would not apply as he is dead.

Assuming a subsequent disposal of the shares at a significant gain this would be outside the scope of UK capital gains tax as the gain would now be realised by a non resident trust.

2. Trusts With All Defined Persons Excluded

Settlements where 'defined persons' are all excluded are difficult to achieve now that the gains of grandchildren's settlements can be attributed to the settlor. But settlements are sometimes made by remote relations or friends of the beneficiaries, and these still operate as a shelter for both income and capital gains.

A particular use may be where assets are expected to increase in value rapidly. The initial funds required may be low and an individual could persuade a friend to contribute the initial funds. Due to the low initial value of the assets there is unlikely to be any inheritance tax payable on the transfer, and any chargeable gain to date could be deferred in terms of Section 260 of the Income and Corporation Taxes Act provided the settlor was not a beneficiary.

If an inheritance tax charge were to arise on the tenth anniversary of the trust, interest in possession (IIP) trusts could be set up to avoid the tax. IIP trusts differ from discretionary trusts in that the beneficiary has a "present right to the present enjoyment" of the trust, as opposed to a discretionary trust where any benefit is at the discretion of the trustees acting in accordance with the trust deed. An IIP trust has a totally different inheritance tax regime and there are some significant capital gains tax and income tax differences as well.

In this case, the settlor would be your friend and you would be the beneficiary.

The anti-avoidance provisions should not apply providing the settlor (in other words, the friend) does not benefit from the trust and he funds the initial cash required out of his own pocket and not under any agreement, eg in order to receive a future benefit.

The trust would therefore be capable of achieving the capital gains tax and income tax advantages mentioned above including an exemption from CGT on a subsequent disposal, without the gain being apportioned back to the UK resident settlor.

3. Children's Settlements

A child's or grandchild's offshore settlement is still an effective shelter of foreign income, although not foreign gains. (This arises as the anti-avoidance provisions applying to capital gains tax are much wider than the income tax provisions). Common assets for the trust to hold would be either shares in a non resident trading company or a portfolio invested abroad for income.

Example

Peter a UK resident and domiciled individual settles cash in an offshore trust for the benefit of his grandchildren who are UK resident. He and his wife are specifically excluded from the class of beneficiaries in the trust deed. The trustees use the cash purchase shares in a UK company. Any dividends received by the offshore trust would not be liable to UK income tax. Clearly if a UK trust was used UK income tax would be fully chargeable on dividends received.

This would then allow a tax-free roll up of funds offshore. If the trust were to pay a distribution to the UK resident grandchildren, UK tax would be payable, although the grandchildren would always have the option of becoming non resident themselves and obtaining the cash free of UK tax during a year of non residency (eg by taking a 'year out').

If the trustees were to sell some of the shares, the gains would be apportioned to Peter as he was the settlor and because the beneficiaries include individuals from an excluded class.

10.7 UK Resident but NOT UK Domiciled

In the absence of a trust the best strategy for a non domiciliary is to keep his investments (along with any income/proceeds) outside the UK. In this way any income tax/capital gains tax liability is avoided under the remittance basis, and inheritance tax only applies to his UK assets/estate.

There are however a number of problems with this approach, in particular, the deemed domicile rules may apply for inheritance tax purposes and treat the individual as UK domiciled for inheritance tax purposes. This would have the effect of subjecting his worldwide estate to UK inheritance tax. There is also, of course, the risk that the individual creates sufficient intention to stay in the UK that he obtains a UK domicile.

Use of a trust could help to avoid these risks. If a non UK domiciliary establishes a trust of which he is a beneficiary, the property in the trust is termed 'excluded property' provided:

- The settlor was not UK domiciled (or deemed domiciled) at the time the trust was established, and

- The trust property is situated outside of the UK.

Example
Terry a UK resident, but of US domicile, has been resident in the UK for 15 years. He owns substantial assets in both the UK and the US and eventually intends to move back to the US and enjoy his retirement. Once Terry has been resident in the UK for 17

years he will have deemed domicile. This will mean that in the event of his untimely death, the whole of his estate would be taxed in accordance with the UK inheritance tax legislation. If Terry was to transfer his non UK assets into a trust now (in other words, before he is deemed UK domiciled), the American assets would be excluded property and outside the scope of UK inheritance tax .

Capital Gains Tax

An excluded property settlement also has a number of advantages from a capital gains tax perspective.

Provided the trustees aren't UK resident and the administration of the trust is carried on overseas, the trust is not subject to UK capital gains tax (unless the UK assets of the trust are used in a UK branch/agency trade).

Tax anti-avoidance rules will attribute the gains of the trust to any UK settlor/beneficiary and the trust gains are treated as their individual gains.

However, when the settlor/beneficiary is non resident or non UK domiciled these rules do not apply and therefore provided the settlor remains non domiciled any trust gains are outside the UK capital gains tax net.

Therefore the use of an overseas trust is expanded for non UK domiciliaries as the anti-avoidance provisions are limited in scope.

The remittance of proceeds would be a capital distribution from the trust to a UK resident individual. The tax treatment of this would depend on how it was structured, and professional advice is essential. A straightforward remittance by a UK resident would be likely to be within the scope of UK tax. One option would be to retain the funds offshore and make a gift to a spouse or other relative. They could then bring the funds into the UK, free of UK capital gains tax and potentially free of UK income tax.

Example

Joe a UK resident, but with Greek domicile settles some assets into an offshore discretionary trust. If the trust later sells the assets at a gain of £1,000,000 there will be no UK capital gains tax charge. The anti avoidance provisions will not attribute the gain to Joe (as he is non UK domiciled) and providing any beneficiaries of the trust are also non UK domiciled, none of the gain will be attributed to them either.

This will apply to both UK and overseas assets settled into the trust.

Income Tax

Again the anti-avoidance provisions are amended, the effect of which is that any UK income of the trust is taxed as the settlor's, whereas foreign income is subject to the remittance basis and will escape UK income tax provided the income is kept overseas by the trustees. If the settlor beneficiary subsequently acquires a UK domicile:

- The inheritance tax position of the trust remains the same (in other words, provided the property is situated overseas, then the trust property is outside the scope of UK inheritance tax).

- For capital gains tax any gains of the trust would become taxed on the settlor as they arise.

- The worldwide income of the trust would be taxed on the settlor.

Example

Eduardo, who was originally born in Latvia, has been UK resident for the last 15 years. He made good use of the benefits of being a non UK domiciliary as regards offshore trusts and has established such trusts which now contain significant assets.

He is in the process of disposing of the last of his Latvian assets and is concerned that given his particular circumstances he may be classed as having UK domicile.

This would be disastrous for Eduardo and income and gains of the trust would be taxable.

In such circumstances, forward thinking is always beneficial.

In the tax year before the change in domicile the trust could distribute sufficient cash to support Eduardo's lifestyle. They would then be excluded from the trust and the anti-avoidance provisions would not attribute income (and gains providing other relevant beneficiaries are excluded) to Eduardo.

Sheltering from Overseas Tax

Dependent on the overseas country's domestic tax rules, using an overseas trust can help to minimise overseas tax, particularly inheritance tax and prevent the establishment of an overseas estate.

Example

David, a non UK domiciliary is considering investing in property in South Africa. If he uses the offshore trust/company structure, the big advantage is that he will not be regarded as owning South African assets. As such he will not be subject to overseas inheritance tax, and will not be subject to the South African estate laws.

10.8 Where Do You Set Up a Trust & How Much Does it Cost?

It is vital when establishing any offshore trusts/companies that they are established in jurisdictions that have a lower level of taxation than the UK.

A selection of the key locations that are commonly preferred when establishing offshore trusts are as follows:

- Channel islands
- Isle of Man
- Liechtenstein
- Bermuda
- Cayman Islands
- Bahamas
- Gibraltar

As well as the taxation regime it is also necessary to consider other factors such as:

- Location (will personal visits be time consuming and telephone contact limited to certain times of day).

- The legal system

- Any political issues

Obviously financial costs are incurred in setting up and running an offshore trust. It is likely to cost from £1,000 + for the initial set up and further charges will be incurred for ongoing compliance work and if you require professional advisers to act as trustees.

Please note that, while there are many reputable firms offering offshore tax planning services, there are also many fly-by-night operators providing advice of dubious quality that may land you in considerable trouble with the UK taxman.

It should also be noted that the settlor and beneficiaries of an offshore trust must disclose all relevant information on their tax returns. In addition, when the trust is established the person making the settlement MUST make a return to Inland Revenue within three months.

Chapter 11

Tax Benefits of Offshore Companies

11.1 Introduction

A UK resident company is subject to UK corporation tax on its worldwide income and gains. By contrast a non UK resident company is only subject to corporation tax on its UK income.

At first glance, therefore, it would seem that an offshore company is an effective way of sheltering income and capital gains from the taxman, as all foreign income and gains accruing to the company should be free of UK tax.

In fact *directly owned* offshore companies have a limited role to play in offshore tax planning. One of the reasons for this is the issue of 'deemed' company residence. A company is regarded as a UK resident if:

- It is a UK incorporated company, or

- Its *central management and control* is in the UK.

Various legal cases have indicated that if the board of directors meet and give proper consideration to any transactions the company undertakes, this will constitute the central management and control. There is a risk that proper procedures may not be followed and in such cases Inland Revenue may argue that the company is run by the controlling shareholder in the UK. In these circumstances the company would be classed as UK resident and subject to UK corporation tax.

11.2 How Inland Revenue Spots Phony Offshore Management

Inland Revenue has stated that it will look at offshore companies to identify if there has been an attempt to create simply the appearance of central management and control in a place.

Therefore, care is needed to ensure that any overseas directors are actually running the company.

In order to pass the central management and control test the majority of the directors should be non UK resident, and the non UK resident directors should actively participate in making board decisions.

This therefore means that key business decisions should be taken at overseas board meetings. A UK resident shareholder may therefore establish a non resident company but it is essential to ensure that the running of the business is left to the non resident directors.

11.3 Apportionment of Capital Gains

UK tax anti-avoidance provisions require the gains of a non-resident 'close' company to be apportioned amongst the member shareholders. Capital gains tax is charged on those who are resident and, in the case of individuals, domiciled in the UK.

The definition of a close company can be complex, however, in simple terms it applies to a company that is controlled by its directors or five or fewer shareholders.

Example

Jack and Jill are the sole shareholders of JackJill Ltd, a company registered in the Cayman Islands. They hold 50% of the shares each and are both UK resident and domiciled. Assuming they allow non resident directors to run the company and can satisfactorily show that the company is not centrally managed and controlled from the UK, then the attribution of gains legislation would mean that any gains of the offshore company would be attributed to Jack and Jill (50% each). However, if Jack was non UK domiciled, the gains would NOT be attributed to him, only to Jill.

11.4 Benefits in Kind

If Inland Revenue are able to assert that the company is being managed by the shareholder or that the directors of the company are accustomed to act on his directions, he will be classed as a shadow director and income tax will be payable on any benefit in kind received by him or his family. One of the key benefits in kind that may apply is the accommodation charge. This levies a charge on an employee where he or she is provided with accommodation by an employer.

11.5 Using a Non Resident Trust & Company

Directly owned offshore companies are not actually that common in practice. Instead offshore companies *owned by offshore trusts* are used more frequently. Such arrangements are often popular from a non tax angle due to the practical advantages of owning the trust investments through one or more wholly owned offshore companies.

The residence of the company is not a key issue in these circumstances as the only persons legally entitled to exercise control of the company are the non resident trustees. However, care would need to be taken to ensure that the company really is run by either the trustees or directors. If they were to stand aside and let a settlor/beneficiary give all the instructions, it could be contended that the company residence is the same as that of the settlor or beneficiary.

Provided the beneficiaries were non resident, they would suffer no UK taxation charge on distributions from the trust, and the company/trust would also suffer no UK tax charge if the assets held were overseas assets.

If the beneficiary is a UK resident, the main problem would be the UK anti-avoidance legislation. There would be no real way of escaping this, although if one of exemptions applied (eg the motive test) satisfied, this could be claimed on the tax return.

The motive test is an important aspect of one of the key anti-avoidance rules that attributes the income of offshore trusts and companies to UK resident individuals. The anti-avoidance provisions will not apply if:

- The avoidance of tax was not the purpose for which the transfer of assets was made, or

- The transfer of assets overseas was a *bona fide* commercial transaction and was not designed for the purpose of avoiding tax.

Therefore for an individual to take advantage of this rule, and claim that income from an offshore company or trust should not be attributed to them, they would need to show that there was no tax avoidance motive in the transfer of any asset overseas and essentially that the companies were located overseas for sound commercial reasons. This can be a difficult provision to satisfy.

In order to be non resident for income tax and capital gains tax purposes the trustees would all need to be non resident and the general administration of the trust would need to be carried on abroad.

Example

Peter, a UK resident and domiciled individual wishes to purchase a business and property in Ibiza. One option would be to establish a trust, and transfer funds to the trustees. They would then either purchase the property directly, or via a wholly owned company.

The transfer of funds from Peter would however, be a problem from an inheritance tax perspective. As Peter is UK domiciled, the settlement is an immediately chargeable transfer, taxable at 20% for amounts above £263,000 (this assumes that he has made no previous gifts).

However, the advantage of using a discretionary trust route is that the property would then be excluded from his estate for inheritance tax purposes. The drawback is that the trust would be subject to a separate regime of UK taxation. For inheritance tax purposes, the trust is subject to UK inheritance tax if Peter was domiciled in the UK when the transfer was made. This would undoubtably be the case.

In these circumstances one option to exempt the trust from UK inheritance tax would be for the transfer to the trust to be of 'relevant business property'. The transfer to the trust would then be exempt from UK inheritance tax, and the trust itself would not suffer an ongoing inheritance tax charge, as business property relief ('BPR') would exclude the property from the inheritance tax charge.

Relevant business property includes a sole trader business, assets used in a partnership and shares in unquoted trading companies. Therefore in this case it would be far better for Peter to purchase the business and property directly and subsequently transfer this to the trust/company.

Provided any transfer was made shortly after transfer, there would be unlikely to be a capital gains tax charge as any increase in value would be minimal. The trust would then be exempt from UK inheritance tax as the assets transferred would qualify for Business Property Relief.

11.6 Using an Offshore Company & Trust: Non UK Domiciliaries

Many non UK domiciliaries, choose to use this structure to minimise their UK tax liabilities.

Example.
Paul is a non UK domiciliary, and wishes to purchase a property in the Isle of Man ('IOM'). He decides to use an offshore company to own the property with 100% of the shares in the company owned by a non- resident IOM trust. The tax implications are as follows:

Capital Gains Tax

As non residents the trust and company will not be subject to UK capital gains tax. Provided the beneficiaries are non UK domiciled any capital gain will not be taxed on distribution to the beneficiary.

Income Tax

Any foreign income earned by the trust is not subject to UK income tax, unless it is remitted to the UK. If the trust/company was to own UK property, the income would however be taxable. The anti avoidance provisions will apply if Paul or his spouse can benefit from the trust. In this case, he will be taxed on the UK income as it arises (whether remitted or not).

Inheritance Tax

The Isle of Man trust is only subject to UK inheritance tax on UK assets, as it was established by a non-UK domiciled individual. By using the offshore company to hold any UK property, there will be no UK inheritance tax on the property, as the trust will hold shares in an IOM company, which are treated as non UK assets for inheritance tax purposes.

Non-UK Domiciled Spouse

Where one spouse is a UK domiciliary, and the other is not, it is still possible for the UK domiciliary's assets to be protected.

In this situation the UK domiciliary could consider transferring assets to the non UK domiciliary. If the £55,000 limit is exceeded, this would be treated as a 'potentially exempt transfer', and therefore exempt from inheritance tax providing the spouse making the gift survives seven years from the date of the transfer.

The non-domiciled spouse could then establish the offshore trust and company structure. The benefits outlined above would then arise. Note that the inter-spouse transfer must not be made subject to any form of condition or immediately prior to the establishment of the offshore structure.

Advanced offshore arrangements should be carefully considered. They frequently involve a complex interaction of many taxation issues, and professional advice will need to be taken.

Chapter 12

Investing in UK Property - Case Study

It is useful to consolidate some of the issues covered above and consider a typical scenario, where a non UK resident and domiciled individual wishes to purchase a UK property.

Jack is resident and domiciled in Spain. He has relatives in the UK and is interested in purchasing a property here because (a) he wants somewhere to stay when he visits and (b) he has heard that UK property prices are set to rise further.

The question is, how from a tax perspective should he structure the purchase?

There are broadly two ways to buy the property:

- By using direct ownership, or

- Some form of intermediary like a trust or company.

12.1 Direct Ownership

Capital Gains Tax

From a capital gains tax perspective direct ownership is potentially attractive:

- The Principal Private Residence (PPR) relief operates to exempt a gain on the disposal of an individual's main residence. Even if the property is not, on the facts, Jacks main residence, he could certainly submit an election to have it treated as his main residence.

- As he is non resident, he would not in any case be liable to UK capital gains tax on the disposal of any assets.

Inheritance Tax

The inheritance tax position is, however, not as good. The holding of property in the UK would mean that Jack has a UK estate and, as well as probate being required on his death, the house would be subject to inheritance tax to the extent that the value exceeds the nil rate band. As the value of the property is expected to rise rapidly, this could result in a significant tax bill were he to die while still owning the asset. There are, however, a number of methods available to Jack to reduce or eliminate any inheritance tax charge:

Use of multiple ownership

The property could be acquired in multiple ownership. For example, Jack, his wife and children could all own the property jointly.

Providing the individuals have no other UK assets, it is likely that each share will be below the nil rate band.

In order to avoid problems with the 'gift with reservation of benefit' legislation, it is necessary to gift cash to the family members, which they can then use to purchase their shares of the property.

The gift with reservation of benefit (GROB) provisions apply to property in particular, where an interest in a property is given away, yet the person gifting the interest still continues to reside in the property. For inheritance tax purposes, the whole value of the property is still regarded as included in the occupier's estate for inheritance tax purposes.

Gifting of property

Another solution would be to gift cash to a younger member of the family who can then make the acquisition. The gift will be exempt from inheritance tax, provided the person making the gift survives seven years. The above GROB rules would not apply as the gift was a cash gift.

The property will then belong to the donee (the younger family member) and if the donee were to die, it would be included in his estate for inheritance tax purposes.

Mortgages

The value of an individual's estate is essentially the market value of the assets at the date of death, less any liabilities outstanding at the date of death.

It is therefore possible to effectively reduce any inheritance tax charge to NIL, by obtaining a substantial loan against the value of the property. Providing the mortgage reduces the 'net value' of the property to below the nil rate band (currently £263,000) there will be no inheritance tax payable.

The mortgage funds obtained can be invested overseas and any interest return would then be exempt from UK income tax providing the interest income is not remitted to the UK.

12.2 Using a Trust to Own the Property

Capital Gains Tax

The Principal Private Residence relief is extended to situations where a beneficiary is entitled to occupy a house under the terms of a trust deed. In these circumstances, the trustees would be able to claim PPR relief when they sell the property.

In the case of a non-UK domiciliary, as the trustees are non resident they would not, in any case, be liable to UK capital gains tax.

It would only be if the settlor of the trust was also a beneficiary and he acquired a UK domicile that the gains of the trust would be attributed to him under the anti-avoidance provisions.

Inheritance tax

If the trust is a discretionary trust (as most are), it will be subject to special inheritance tax rules. One of the key implications is that it could be subject to an inheritance tax charge every ten years starting with the date of commencement.

A more serious problem is that Inland Revenue could contend that the non domiciliary has a 'notional interest in possession' in the property. This is a complex area, however the result of the authorities being successful in this argument would be that the value of the property would be included within the occupier's estate on his death (similar to the effect of the GROB provisions).

One method of avoiding this would be to grant a tenancy at a low or nominal rent.

12.3 Using an Offshore Company

The property could be owned by a non resident company. In this case the non domiciliary would own the shares in the company.

As the shares are non UK property, they would be exempt from inheritance tax. Key risks with this are:

- The company's residence position may be closely scrutinised by the taxman and it may be difficult to show that the central management and control is exercised outside the UK, particularly if all directors are UK resident and the asset of the company is a UK property.

  If Inland Revenue was able to successfully argue that the company is UK resident, any gain on the disposal of the property would be subject to UK corporation tax and no PPR relief would be available.

- In addition, on disposal of the shares in the company, no capital gains tax would be payable by the non domiciliary providing the proceeds were retained outside of the UK - again this could be challenged by Inland Revenue by arguing that the central management and control of the company occurred in the UK.

12.4 Conclusion

Deciding how a non domiciliary should own UK property is clearly not a straightforward decision.

Much will depend on the particular circumstances and your personal preferences. For example, you may be more anxious to avoid capital gains tax than inheritance tax.

To a certain extent the simplest route - direct ownership - offers some important tax advantages providing potential inheritance tax can be avoided in some way, for example, by using debt.

Chapter 13

Becoming a Tax Nomad

Just as it is possible to be resident in more than one country, it is also possible to be resident in none. Such individuals are commonly known as 'tax nomads'.

If you become a tax nomad you would still be liable for income tax on any income generated within a particular country, but *capital gains tax* usually depends on the concept of residence.

In order to achieve your objective and pay no capital gains tax, you will need to ensure that you have a thorough understanding of the relevant countries domestic tax laws, as well as the impact of any double taxation treaties.

The definition of residence varies significantly. Some countries, such as the UK and Ireland, have an objective test, which is determined by the number of days spent within the country.

Other countries, such as France and Germany, have a more subjective test that is based on where an individual's 'centre of economic interest' is located or the place of 'habitual abode'.

Example

Jack spends his time during the tax year 2004/2005 as follows:

- *127 days in Ireland,*

- *84 days a year in the UK,*

- *110 days in the USA,*

- *The remainder of the year on holiday in the Maldives.*

He would not be resident in any of the above countries for tax purposes and this would allow him to avoid a potentially large gain on a disposal of his investment property.

Moving abroad may offer an opportunity to wash out gains in your investment portfolio tax-free, since it may be possible to arrange your move so that for a period you are 'resident nowhere'. For example, if you move to Spain and leave the UK on 5 April 2005 and travel via France, arriving in Spain on 10 April 2005, any capital gains you realise during the four day 'tax holiday' between these dates will be free of capital gains tax (unless you resume tax residence in the UK within five years).

Whilst becoming a tax nomad may not be a suitable option long term, it could prove useful for one or two years – it allows you to structure your affairs before taking up residence in a country of your choice.

Chapter 14

Double Tax Treaties

14.1 How Double Tax Treaties Work

The rules detailed earlier in this guide explain the concepts of 'residence', 'ordinary residence' and 'domicile' and identify when an individual will be liable to pay UK tax as a result of being resident/ordinarily resident in this country.

But an individual may also be regarded as resident in another country according to its tax laws. This is where double tax treaties come into play.

A double tax treaty is essentially an agreement between two countries that will determine which country has the right to tax you in specified situations. The purpose is to avoid double taxation.

The UK has double tax treaties with a number of countries including popular retirement destinations such as Spain, Portugal, Italy and France.

The majority of the UK's double tax treaties are based on the 'standard' provisions in the model treaty of the Organisation for Economic Cooperation and Development (OECD).

This includes a 'tie-breaker' clause that effectively overrides the two countries' domestic laws and makes the individual resident in one country only.

The terms of double tax treaties can be immensely complex, although on a simple level they can provide for one country to have primary taxing rights over certain sources of income and gains.

The OECD model treaty provides that:

- If you have a permanent home in one state, you are resident in that state.

- If you have a permanent home in both states, you are resident in the state which is your 'centre of vital interests' - the country in which you have close personal and financial ties.

- If you do not have a permanent home in either state and it is not possible to determine your centre of vital interests, you are resident in the country where you have an 'habitual abode'.

One important point to note is that there are very few low tax countries that have double tax treaties with this country. The UK has, however, concluded double tax treaties with the Channel Islands and the Isle of man, which are low tax jurisdictions. The UK-Isle of Man double tax treaty is looked at in more detail below.

It is also crucial to note that for a double tax treaty to apply, you must be resident in two countries under the terms of each country's domestic laws. The treaty cannot make you resident in a country if you are not already resident under the domestic law of that country.

14.2 Review of the UK-Isle of Man Double Tax Treaty

The Isle of Man (IOM) only has one Double Taxation Agreement which was entered into with the United Kingdom in 1955 and is very similar to agreements drawn up between the UK and Jersey and Guernsey.

The treaty does not conform to the OECD standard model treaty and is of limited scope. The main features that may be of interest are the following:

- The agreement applies only for income tax purposes (in both the IOM and the UK).

- An individual resident in only one of the two countries is exempt from tax in the other country on personal, including professional, services performed in the other country on behalf of a resident of his own country (but they must be taxed in his own country). In other words, if you were a resident of the IOM and performed services in the UK for a UK resident individual, then providing the income was taxed in the IOM, there would be no UK tax liability.

If these criteria are not met then tax would be payable in both countries, although the tax paid in one country is allowed as a credit against tax due in the other. If you did incur UK tax whilst being an IOM resident, the UK tax paid would be offset against any IOM tax.

Given that UK income tax rates are generally significantly higher then IOM rates, this would extinguish any IOM income tax liability.

- It is important to note that capital gains tax is not subject to the double tax treaty.

14.3 Why the Isle of Man is so Attractive

Tax rates are much lower in the Isle of Man than in the UK.

Income tax is levied at a rate of only 10% on the first £10,000 of taxable income and 18% on the rest. Individuals receive an £8,000 personal allowance. Married couples are taxed jointly and receive a personal allowance of £16,000, pay 10% on the first £20,000 of taxable income and 18% on the rest.

National Insurance is a form of social security taxation. It is levied on employment income at an identical rate to the UK. For employees the rate is 11% on income between £91 and £610 per week.

Rates are a form of property tax and are based on a notional house value multiplied by a formula set by the local authority.

VAT is charged at 17.5% on the value of an item. There are some variations, but generally the tax is applied in a similar manner to the UK.

There is no capital gains tax in the Isle of Man.

14.4 How to Become Resident in the Isle of Man

There is no general definition of 'residence' or 'ordinary residence' in Manx tax law - these terms are often interpreted in the same way as in English law.

A person will qualify as a resident if he spends a total of 6 months on the island in any income tax year (April 6th to April 5th). An individual who visits for more than an average of three months each year for four or more consecutive years will also be deemed resident. There is an important short term residence concession which allows a person who owns a property on the island to spend not more than four months in any two consecutive years in the island and not be liable to Manx income tax.

A new resident is taxed from the date of his arrival, while a person who leaves is non-resident from the date of departure. Resident individuals are liable to tax on their worldwide income; non residents only on income arising in the island.

14.5 How Double Tax Treaties Can be Used to Save Tax

Much depends on the terms of the particular treaty so it is worthwhile having both the domestic taxation regime and any double tax treaty reviewed prior to leaving the country.

Many property investors are interested in using a company structure to avoid tax and it is frequently suggested that an overseas company can be used to avoid capital gains tax.

There are a number of risks with using an offshore company as mentioned earlier. One of the major problems is that gains of the offshore company can be apportioned to any UK resident and domiciled shareholders.

However, certain tax treaties that the UK has drawn up with other countries, including the Netherlands, Belgium and Luxembourg, effectively prevent these provisions from applying to companies resident in those jurisdictions, although the rules will still apply to gains on the sale of land/property.

Example
Suppose Neil wants to buy a significant amount of investment property. Neil is resident and domiciled in the UK.

Neil is advised to form an offshore company in Belgium. This company owns another company (in, say, the Isle of man). The Isle of Man company purchases property in the UK.

If the shares in the Isle of Man company are sold, as opposed to the actual property, any gain arising would generally be prevented from being apportioned back to the UK shareholders under the tax anti-avoidance legislation. Of course, it would still be possible for the taxman to argue that the companies are UK resident under the central management and control test. It would therefore be necessary to appoint overseas directors who are given considerable autonomy in decision making.

By using the two-company structure and taking advantage of the favourable UK-Belgium double tax treaty, the gain arising on the sale of the shares would be outside the scope of UK capital gains tax, even if a <u>UK resident individual owned shares in the Belgian company.</u>

As we know offshore planning for UK residents is difficult given the raft of anti-avoidance rules in place. However, this is a good example of how an offshore company structure can be used to minimise any UK tax liability.

14.6 Treaty Relief

Remember that double tax treaties override domestic tax legislation, and will therefore overrule the domestic tax rules. In the standard OECD model tax treaty, dividends are taxed in the country of residence, as opposed to the country where the company is resident.

Example
Peter is a resident of South Africa. He holds shares in a UK resident company and receives dividends twice yearly (interim and final dividends). Under the UK - South Africa double tax treaty, the dividends will be taxed solely in South Africa.

Similarly, interest is also taxed in the country where the individual is resident. Therefore, if in the above example Peter received interest from a UK bank, as a South African resident the treaty now exempts the UK source interest from UK tax.

However, interest is automatically paid net, as income tax of 20% is withheld. In this case, you would need to contact the Inland Revenue and treaty relief will need to be applied for in order that the exemption from UK tax can apply. This would then allow a repayment of any tax withheld, and would ensure that no income tax is deducted on future payments.

Claiming treaty relief can be a long process. The form, which can be obtained from the Inland Revenue, must be completed and passed to the overseas revenue service. They will then review the information and pass this to the UK Inland Revenue where the Centre for Non Residents will issue a certificate granting relief.

14.7 Considering a Move to Spain

Let's have a look at Spain, a popular destination for potential expats. Whilst Spain does not offer low tax rates, it still remains a popular choice for UK emigrants due to its proximity to the UK, fantastic climate and political stability.

Those who either purchase Spanish assets or acquire Spanish residence will be affected by the local tax regime so it's worth examining in greater detail.

We shall give a brief overview of the Spanish tax regime below. This will highlight the similarities and differences between the two countries, before looking at how the UK-Spain double tax treaty affects matters.

Residence
The extent that you are liable to these taxes will depend on your residence position. You will either be UK resident or Spanish resident (assuming you live and split your time between the UK and Spain).

Why does residence matter?
The short answer is that UK and Spanish residents are taxed on their *worldwide* income and gains, whereas non residents are

only liable to tax on the income arising *within* that particular country. For example, non UK residents are only liable to UK income tax on their UK income.

Spanish residence

The first point to note is that the Spanish tax year is based on calendar years, unlike our tax year which runs from 6th April to 5th April. There are numerous rules regarding different levels of status in Spain:

- Individuals who spend more than 183 days in Spain during one calendar year must apply for a Spanish resident card, and be classed as permanent residents. These days do not have to be consecutive. You do not become a resident for tax purposes until the morning of the 184th day.

- Temporary absences from Spain are ignored for the purpose of this rule unless it can be proved that the individual is habitually resident in another country for more than 183 days in a calendar year.

- If you arrive in Spain with the intention of living there indefinitely, the Spanish tax authorities (known as the 'Hacienda') will treat you as Spanish resident from the day after your arrival.

- If your spouse lives in Spain, you will be presumed to be a resident of Spain, providing you are not separated/divorced even though you may actually spend less than 183 days per year in Spain.

- If you spend more than 90 days in Spain, you would need to apply for a temporary resident card, which would essentially allow you a further 90 days in Spain. If you wished to stay longer than this you would need to apply to stay as a permanent resident, as above.

If you live on a boat within 12 nautical miles of Spanish land, you are classed as a Spanish tax resident. A day within 12 nautical miles is a day spent in Spain for tax purposes.

It is clear that following the UK and Spanish domestic residence rules (above) an individual can be resident in both the UK and Spain. This is where it is important to identify how the double taxation agreement regulates matters.

How does the UK/Spain Tax Treaty affect matters?

The UK/Spain Double Tax Treaty has a 'tie-breaker' clause that comes into effect if an individual is classed as resident in the UK and Spain (under the domestic rules outlined above). This clause determines which country is to be given sole taxing rights, and prevents an individual being subject to UK and Spanish taxes on the same income. The double tax agreement states that:

- If an individual is resident in both Spain and the UK, according to the domestic tax rules, he is to be deemed resident in the country in which he has a permanent home.

- If he has permanent homes in both Spain and the UK, he is deemed to be resident in the country that is classed as his centre of vital interests. This is a vague term, although it is generally regarded as the country with which an individual has the strongest ties and will therefore include both personal and financial connections.

- If it is still not possible to determine which country has the taxing rights, it is necessary to look at the individual's habitual abode – the country in which he has his habitual abode (which is similar to the concept of main residence) will be his country of residence.

- If he has an habitual abode in the UK and Spain, he will be resident in the country in which he is a national.

Example

Bob, a UK resident, owns a villa in Spain. If he occupies the villa for 3 months he will be a UK (not Spanish) resident, liable to UK income tax. If Bob rents out the villa, both the UK and Spanish tax authorities are likely to become interested. Although non resident in Spain, Bob's rental income will have a Spanish source and so Spanish tax will be payable. The UK tax authorities will be interested because Bob is UK resident, therefore subject to UK income tax on his worldwide income. In this case, the UK-Spain double tax treaty allows both countries the right to tax the income, so Bob will pay UK income tax and Spanish income tax (at the non resident rate of 25% on the gross income, with no deductions for expenses or interest costs). Bob needs to keep copies of his Spanish tax returns, so he can offset the Spanish tax against any UK liability. Assume that Bob is a UK higher rate taxpayer, and receives rental income of £10,000 and incurs costs of £2,000.The Spanish income tax liability would be £2,500 (£10,000 x 25%). UK tax would be 10,000 - £2,000 x 40% = £3,200.

Bob would then be entitled to deduct the Spanish income tax paid from the UK income tax. The net effect of this is that Bob would actually pay £3,200 in income tax on the villa (£2,500 in Spain and £700 in the UK).

What else does the double tax treaty say?

The treaty has specific rules that will apply to certain types of income, irrespective of the domestic tax laws of UK or Spain.

Under the domestic tax legislation of the UK and Spain it is easily possible for an individual to be classed as resident in both countries simultaneously. The individual would then be subject to both UK and Spanish tax on the same income. This is clearly inequitable, and both the UK and Spain provide for a system of double tax relief where there is an element of double taxation.

However, in order to minimise this double taxation the treaty has specifically stated in which country certain types of income will be taxed, when both countries may have a claim on the same income. The summarised rules are as follows:

Rental income

The general rule is that this is taxed in country where the property is situated. Therefore once you become a resident in Spain, you will still have to pay income tax on the rental income you derive from your UK property to the UK Inland Revenue. This means that you would pay tax in the UK and not in Spain. The non-resident landlord scheme, which forces tenants and letting agents to pay over tax on behalf of overseas property owners, would then apply.

Dividend income, interest income & pension income

This is taxed in the country where the shareholder is resident. Therefore a Spanish resident individual receiving dividend income from a UK resident company would pay income tax in Spain under the terms of the double taxation agreement.

Capital gains on disposal of property

This is taxed in the country where the property is situated.
Therefore a Spanish resident disposing of a UK property would be exempt from UK capital gains tax provided they satisfied the UK rules (for example, non resident & ordinarily resident for five complete tax years).

You will see that whilst the domestic concepts of residence for UK and Spain are important, the double tax treaty certainly simplifies matters, as it basically tells us which countries rules to use. When considering a move to any country you should consider whether a double tax treaty exist and how this will impact on the tax treatment of income and gains.

Chapter 15

Buying Property Abroad

15.1 Introduction

British winters tend to make people dream about their next holiday. Some of you will be considering going one step further and actually purchasing a property overseas. Property prices on the Spanish costas for example have been rising at 10-15% per year in recent times and can make a good investment, as well as providing an opportunity to catch up on your sun tan!

There is a tendency for people purchasing such properties to get caught up in the various legal formalities and excitement of owning an overseas property, and neglect to have a good look into how the property, including any income and capital gains will be taxed.

The UK tax treatment will depend primarily on the tax status of the purchaser. Let's have a look at the UK tax implications for different types of purchaser, pooling together what we've learned from the previous chapters.

15.2 UK Resident/Ordinarily Resident and Domiciled

Any income and gains arising from the property will in the first instance be liable to UK taxes in full. The property will also be included within your estate for inheritance tax purposes.

Example

Jake is resident and domiciled in the UK. He decides to purchase a property in Latvia for letting during the summer months, and for his own occupation during the winter. The rental income will be subject to UK income tax. Any gain/profit on a subsequent disposal will be liable to UK capital gains tax (less various reliefs). If he was to die whilst still owning the Latvian property, this would be taken into account when assessing the amount of inheritance tax he would pay.

15.3 Non Resident/Ordinarily Resident and Non UK Domiciled

As you would expect, as a non resident, any income and gains from the overseas property will not be liable to UK taxes. Similarly, the property would not be included within the individual's estate for inheritance tax purposes.

Example

Jacob, originally born in Portugal has lived in Spain for 15 years and is regarded as non UK resident and non UK domiciled. His Spanish property would not be subject to UK taxes.

Note that for capital gains tax purposes, an individual must be non resident for 5 complete tax years before being exempted from UK capital gains tax on assets held at the date of their emigration.

This provision was enacted in 1998 to prevent people with large potential gains in assets, becoming non resident for a tax year, disposing of the asset and avoiding UK capital gains tax.

15.4 UK Resident/Ordinarily Resident and Non UK Domiciled

Individuals who are UK resident but non UK domiciled have a number of advantages as regards UK taxes. Such individuals are typically foreign nationals, usually born overseas, who have come to live in the UK for a number of years.

The key aspect will be that for income tax and capital gains tax the remittance basis applies. This means that, any rental income obtained from the overseas property would be exempt from UK taxes provided the income was not remitted to the UK. In addition on a future disposal, no UK capital gains tax would be charged provided the proceeds of disposal were retained overseas.

Again, from a UK tax perspective, there would be no UK inheritance tax impact. As a non UK domiciliary, your estate would include only UK assets.

Example

Petra has lived in the UK for 10 years, but has retained her overseas domicile. Petra has purchased a property in Monaco. She plans to let this for 2 years and then dispose of it for a (hopefully!) significant profit.

Provided Petra retains the income overseas (eg, in an offshore bank account) and doesn't bring it into the UK, there will be no UK income tax charge. The same principle will apply to the sale proceeds.

This will allow Petra to build up a tax-free amount that she could use to purchase further offshore properties.

Similarly, the property would not be classed as part of Petra's estate for inheritance tax purposes (being non UK property of a non UK domiciliary).

One point to watch out for are the 'deemed domicile' rules. These apply for inheritance tax purposes only and state that individuals are deemed to have a UK domicile:

- If they have been UK resident for 17 out of the last 20 years, or

- They have lost their UK domicile in the last 3 years.

Example
In the above example, assume Petra has been living in the UK since 1970.

For income tax purposes and capital gains tax purposes, Petra is of non UK domicile. However, for inheritance tax purposes, she is deemed UK domicile as she has lived in the UK since 1970 and would therefore have been resident for more than 17 years.

Therefore for inheritance tax purposes, Petra's estate would be subject to UK inheritance tax on her worldwide estate. This would mean that the property in Monaco could be potentially subject to UK Inheritance tax.

Non UK domiciliaries have a useful tax advantage when considering investing in overseas property. Provided they reinvest income/proceeds offshore, they can avoid UK taxes. This could result in a significant increase in the size and value of their investment portfolios as it enables them to reinvest in more overseas properties. This can give a useful boost to an offshore property portfolio.

15.5 Use of an Offshore Company/Trust

A common misconception is that an offshore company or trust can be used in virtually all situations to avoid UK taxes. Unfortunately this is not true. For UK resident and domiciled individuals the UK tax authorities have a number of powerful anti avoidance measures at their disposal.

This essentially allows the taxman to deem income to be subject to UK tax, or arise on the UK resident shareholder/beneficiary in a number of situations. It is therefore only in a number of limited situations that UK residents and domiciliaries can use offshore companies/trusts to avoid UK taxes.

Non UK domiciliaries can, however, make good use of offshore trusts to purchase overseas property. The trust would not be subject to UK inheritance tax as the assets of the trust would be overseas assets.

From a capital gains tax perspective, the trustees would not be liable to UK capital gains tax, as the trust would be non resident. Providing the creator of the trust retains his non UK domicile status, the UK anti avoidance provisions attributing/deeming gains would not apply.

Providing the overseas jurisdiction does not levy capital gains tax, there would also be no overseas tax charge (eg, the Isle of Man).

Another useful opportunity for the non UK domiciliary is to ensure that UK assets are owned by a non resident company, of which the non domiciliary is a 100% shareholder.

This would then ensure that the individual owns offshore assets (exempt from inheritance tax for non UK domiciliaries) as opposed to UK assets (charged to UK inheritance tax).

15.6 What about Overseas Tax Implications?

Of course the downside to all of the above is that we have only looked at the UK tax implications. Many countries retain the right to tax:

- Residents, and
- Assets of non residents located within their jurisdiction.

Therefore, anyone considering purchasing a property overseas should take advice from a relevant tax professional as to how any income or gain will be taxed.

In the case of Spain, for example, UK resident individuals are be taxed at a standard 35% on any gains arising on a disposal and 25% on the gross rental income from a Spanish property.

In addition, the 'standard' double tax treaty that most countries choose to adopt would treat the income/gain as being sourced from the country where it is located and therefore subject to the overseas tax regime. It would therefore only be if a property was purchased in a 'tax haven' that liability could be avoided.

Such tax havens include Andorra, Monaco, and the Cayman Islands.

15.7 Double Tax Relief (DTR)

If you are subject to tax both in the UK and overseas, there are provisions designed to ensure that you don't pay tax twice. As mentioned earlier this is known as DTR and you can claim DTR against your UK tax charge.

DTR is given as the lower of:

- The UK tax on the overseas income

- The overseas tax

Therefore, if the overseas tax was charged at 50%, with UK being 40%. You would obtain DTR at 40%. Similarly, if the overseas tax was charged at 20%, and UK tax 40%, you would only obtain DTR at 20%. The net effect of this is that you will be left paying the highest tax charge.

Example
Richard, a UK resident individual has the following income in the 2004/2005 tax year:

UK Salary	£40,000
UK dividends (Gross)	£2,000
Overseas rental income	£3,000
(50% overseas tax paid)	

His tax calculation would be:

Salary from UK employment	£40,000
Overseas income	£3,000
UK dividends	£2,000
Less personal allowance	(£4,745)
Taxable income	£40,255

The income tax levied on this taxable income would be reduced by double tax relief.

As the overseas income will be subject to tax at the higher rate (as the taxable income exceeds the UK higher rate tax band), we can calculate that the double tax relief will be the lower of

- *The UK tax on overseas income (40% x £3,000) = £1,200*

- *The overseas tax (50% x £3,000) = £1,500*

Therefore total double tax relief in this case would be £1,200 (lowest of the two figures) and this would be given as a credit against Richard's tax liability.

15.8 Summary

The tax implications of purchasing a property overseas are certainly not straightforward, and you should always consider carefully the UK (and just as importantly) the overseas tax implications.

By way of a summary, I would suggest that the following points be borne in mind when purchasing a property overseas:

- Assess your residence/domicile position to ascertain your liability to UK taxes.

- Obtain overseas tax advice to determine what rate of taxes (if any!) exist overseas.

- Retain all receipts (eg conveyancing fees, valuations, agency fees) - these can be offset when calculating any gain charged to UK capital gains tax.

- Keep full information/documentation of any tax suffered on overseas income/gains - this will be required to substantiate a DTR claim, should the Inland Revenue ask questions after you submit your tax return.

- Think about the most effective structure for the purchase, whether this be by you individually or via a company or trust.

- If you are a non UK domiciliary, watch out for the deemed domicile rules, and consider establishing an offshore trust, sooner rather than later. It is the status of the trust creator at the date the trust was established that is crucial for inheritance tax purposes. If you later became a UK domiciliary, the trust assets would still be exempt from UK inheritance tax.

Appendix: UK-Spain Double Tax Treaty

Article 13 UK Spain Double Tax Treaty

(1) Capital gains from the alienation of immovable property, as defined in paragraph (2) of Article 6, may be taxed in the Contracting State in which such property is situated.

(2) Capital gains from the alienation of movable property forming part of the business property of a permanent establishment which an enterprise of a Contracting State has in the other Contracting State or of movable property pertaining to a fixed base available to a resident of a Contracting State in the other Contracting State for the purpose of performing professional services, including such gains from the alienation of such a permanent establishment (alone or together with the whole enterprise) or of such a fixed base, may be taxed in the other State.

(3) Notwithstanding the provisions of paragraph (2) of this Article, capital gains derived by a resident of a Contracting State from the alienation of ships and aircraft operated in international traffic and movable property pertaining to the operation of such ships and aircraft shall be taxable only in that Contracting State.

(4) Capital gains from the alienation of any property other than those mentioned in paragraphs (1), (2) and (3) of this Article shall be taxable only in the Contracting State of which the alienator is a resident.

Article 24(4)

Income and capital gains owned by a resident of a Contracting State which may be taxed in the other Contracting State in accordance with this Convention shall be deemed to arise from sources in that other Contracting State.

Need Affordable & Expert Tax Planning Advice?

Try Our Unique Question & Answer Service

The purpose of this guide is to provide you with detailed guidance on how to pay less UK tax if you become non-resident or use offshore tax planning techniques.

Ultimately you may want to take further action or obtain advice personal to your circumstances.

Taxcafe.co.uk has a unique online tax advice service that provides access to highly qualified tax professionals at an affordable rate.

No matter how complex your question, we will provide you with detailed tax planning guidance through this service. The cost is just £69.95.

To find out more go to **www.taxcafe.co.uk** and click the Tax Questions button.

Pay Less Tax!

... with help from Taxcafe's unique tax guides and software

<u>All products available online at</u> **www.taxcafe.co.uk**

- **Incorporate & Save Tax**. Everything you need to know about the tax benefits of using a company to run your business.

- **How to Avoid Property Tax.** Essential reading for property investors who want to know all the tips and tricks to follow to pay less tax on their property profits.

- **Using a Property Company to Save Tax.** How to massively increase your profits by using a property company... plus all the traps to avoid.

- **How to Avoid Inheritance Tax**. A-Z of inheritance tax planning, with clear explanations & numerous examples. Covers simple & sophisticated tax planning.

- **Non Resident & Offshore Tax Planning**. How to exploit non resident tax status to reduce your tax bill, plus advice on using offshore trusts and companies.

- **Bonus vs Dividends.** Shows how shareholder/directors of companies can save thousands in tax by choosing the optimal mix of bonus and dividends.

- **Selling a Business.** A potential minefield with numerous traps to avoid but significant tax saving opportunities.

- **How to Claim Tax Credits.** Even families with higher incomes can make successful tax credit claims. This guide shows how much you can claim and how to go about it.

- **Property Capital Gains Tax Calculator.** Unique software that performs complex capital gains tax calculations in seconds.

- **Fast Tax Advice**. We offer a unique Tax Question Service. Answers from highly qualified specialist tax advisers. Just click the Tax Questions button on our site.

Essential Property Investment Guides

...written by leading experts and packed with tips & tricks of the trade

All products available online at www.taxcafe.co.uk

- **An Insider's Guide to Successful Property Investing.** Little-known secrets of successful property investors. A 'must read' for anyone interested in making big profits and avoiding costly mistakes.

- **An Insider's Guide - Part II.** How the experts make millions by using simple but clever techniques to find, buy, manage and sell property.

- **No Money Down Property Millions.** Written by a wealthy property investor, this entertaining and brilliantly clever guide shows you how to invest in property without using any of your own money.

- **The Successful Landlord's Handbook.** Definitive guide for Buy to Let investors. Covers: sourcing cheap property, using borrowed money to earn big capital gains, finding quality tenants, legal traps, letting agents, and lots more...

- **63 Common Defects in Investment Property & How to Spot Them.** With full colour illustrations, this unique guide will save you thousands by steering you clear of no-hope property investments and towards bargain-priced gems.

- **Property Auctions Bargains**. One of the best-kept secrets of successful property investors is to buy at rock-bottom prices at auction. This A-Z guide reveals all.

DISCLAIMER BY TAXCAFE UK LIMITED

Printed in the United Kingdom
by Lightning Source UK Ltd.
105398UKS00002B/41-46